Reporting in TFS

Create and customize reports in Team Foundation
Server using Excel and SQL Server Reporting Services

Dipti Chhatrapati

BIRMINGHAM - MUMBAI

Reporting in TFS

First published: April 2015

Production reference: 1010415

Published by Packt Publishing Ltd.
Livery Place
35 Livery Street
Birmingham B3 2PB, UK.

ISBN 978-1-78217-613-8

www.packtpub.com

Credits

Author
Dipti Chhatrapati

Reviewers
Carlos Hulot

Tarkan Karadayi

Mathias Olausson

Umesh Pandit

Ankit Pradhan

Ariel Woscoboinik

Commissioning Editor
Amarabha Banerjee

Acquisition Editor
Subho Gupta

Content Development Editor
Manasi Pandire

Technical Editor
Rohith Rajan

Copy Editors
Deepa Nambiar

Shambhavi Pai

Project Coordinator
Leena Purkait

Proofreaders
Stephen Copestake

Maria Gould

Indexer
Tejal Soni

Production Coordinator
Melwyn D'sa

Cover Work
Melwyn D'sa

About the Author

Dipti Chhatrapati is a Microsoft SharePoint specialist and is currently working as a senior consultant at Capgemini in Mumbai, India. She has more than 7 years of experience in application development, design, maintenance, and administration and is continuously working to improve her skills and keeping them up to date. As a developer and project leader, she has been an extensive user of Microsoft Visual Studio and Team Foundation Server throughout her career. Dipti blogs at www. sharepointrun.com and can be reached on Twitter at @dips84 and via e-mail at diptichhatrapati@gmail.com. Dipti is very passionate about music, sports, and arts, and loves to spend her free time learning new things, socializing with friends and family, cooking, exercising, and singing.

My deepest thanks to SharePoint MVP, Bjorn H Rapp, for mentoring and correcting me in various skills, areas of knowledge, and platforms with attention and care.

I express hearty thanks to my mother, Rekhaben Chhatrapati, and other family members as well as my close friends, who encouraged me to write this book.

About the Reviewers

Carlos Hulot has been working in the IT area for more than 20 years in different areas, from software development and project management to IT, marketing, product development, and management. He has worked for multinational companies such as Royal Philips Electronics and PriceWaterhouseCoopers. Currently, Carlos is working at Microsoft as an enterprise architect. Carlos was a computer science lecturer at two Brazilian universities. Carlos holds a PhD in computer science and electronics from the University of Southampton, UK, and a BSc degree in physics from the University of São Paulo, Brazil.

> I would like to thank my wife, Mylene Melly, for her continuous support. I also would like to thank my many colleagues over the years who have made it possible for me to learn what I know now about software development and the computer industry.

Tarkan Karadayi has been a professional software developer for over 15 years. He has a master's degree in computer science and is currently working as a principal software engineer.

> I would like to thank my wife, Anna, and my sons, Taran, Kyle, and Ryan, for their love and support.

Mathias Olausson works as the CTO and ALM practice lead at Solidify and specializes in software craftsmanship and Application Life Cycle Management. With over 15 years of experience as a software consultant and trainer, he has worked in numerous projects and organizations, which has been very useful when using Visual Studio as a tool to improve the way we build software. Olausson has been a Microsoft Visual Studio ALM MVP for 6 years. He is also active as a Visual Studio ALM Ranger and most recently in the role of project lead for the Visual Studio Lab Management Guide project. Olausson is a frequent speaker on Visual Studio and Team Foundation Server at conferences and industry events.

He has written *Pro Application Lifecycle Management with Visual Studio 2012* and *Pro Team Foundation Service*, both published by Apress Media LLC.

Umesh Pandit is a Microsoft Dynamics AX deployment senior specialist and currently works with Hitachi Solutions India. He has a master's degree in computer applications with a first division in specialization in ERP from Ideal Institute of Technology, Ghaziabad.

Umesh is a Microsoft Certified Professional for Microsoft Dynamics AX 2009 Installation and Configuration, Microsoft Dynamics AX 2012 Installation and Configuration, Server Virtualization with Windows Server Hyper-V and System Center, Microsoft Dynamics AX 2012 Development Introduction Part 1, Microsoft Dynamics POS 2009, administering Microsoft SQL Server 2012 Databases, and implementing Microsoft Azure infrastructure solutions.

In the past, he successfully reviewed *Microsoft Dynamics AX 2012 Reporting Cookbook* by Kamalakannan Elamgovan, *Developing SSRS Reports for Dynamics AX* by Mukesh Hirwani, and *Microsoft Dynamics AX 2012 Programming: Getting Started* by Mohammed Rasheed and Erlend Dalen, all by Packt Publishing.

He has worked with top IT giants such as KPIT Technologies, Capgemini India, Google India, and a cable manufacturing company called Cords Cable Industries.

Umesh has a deep understanding of ERP systems such as Microsoft Dynamics AX and SAP. He has worked with different versions of Microsoft Dynamics AX, starting with Axapta versions such as AX 3.0, AX 4.0, AX 2009, AX 2012, AX 2012 R2, AX 2012 R3, and AX 2012 R3 CU8. He has a vast knowledge of Microsoft Technologies such as SQL 2014, CRM, TFS, Office 2013, Windows Server 2003, Window Server 2008, Windows Server 2012, Office 365, Microsoft Dynamics NAV, SSRS, Cubes, Management Reporter, SSAS, and Visual Studio.

He can be reached at `pandit.umesh@hotmail.com` and he blogs at: `http://msdynamicsaxtips.blogspot.in/`.

I would like to give special thanks to my close friend, Pramila, who supported me a lot, and best buddies at work: Sunil Wadhwa, Rohan Sodani, Fareeda Begum, Aman Bhatia, Gyan Chand Kabra, Debashish Ray, Arjita Choudhury, and Meenakshi Pandey, who have guided me and encouraged my passion.

Ankit Pradhan is a technology enthusiast with years of experience in design and architecture of large-scale SOA and advanced analytic solutions for major financial and telecom companies in the Americas and EMEA regions.

Besides his experience on the technological front, he has also led Agile-based transformations programs and established Distributed Agile Development factories for a number of organizations.

He holds a bachelor's degree in computer science and a post graduate diploma in business administration with finance as his major.

Ariel Woscoboinik graduated as a bachelor of information technology from the University of Buenos Aires and as an IT technician from ORT schools. Since his childhood, he has been programing and getting more and more involved in the world of technology. Later on, he became interested in organizations and their business models and succeeded in converging both interests into his career: looking for the best solutions to involve people, processes, and technology.

Currently, he works as a software development manager for Telefe, the leading TV channel in Argentina.

Ariel had been working with Microsoft technologies since high school. During his career, he has worked for highly prestigious companies from a plethora of industries such as Microsoft, MAE, Intermex LLC, Pfizer, Monsanto, Banco Santander, IHSA, Disco S.A., Grupo Ecosistemas, Perception Group, Awabee, and Pirca Solutions.

His passions include drama, acting, film-watching, soccer, and traveling around the world.

He recently got married to Lara Barneda.

www.PacktPub.com

Support files, eBooks, discount offers, and more

For support files and downloads related to your book, please visit www.PacktPub.com.

Did you know that Packt offers eBook versions of every book published, with PDF and ePub files available? You can upgrade to the eBook version at www.PacktPub.com and, as a print book customer, you are entitled to a discount on the eBook copy. Get in touch with us at service@packtpub.com for more details.

At www.PacktPub.com, you can also read a collection of free technical articles, sign up for a range of free newsletters, and receive exclusive discounts and offers on Packt books and eBooks.

https://www2.packtpub.com/books/subscription/packtlib

Do you need instant solutions to your IT questions? PacktLib is Packt's online digital book library. Here, you can search, access, and read Packt's entire library of books.

Why subscribe?
- Fully searchable across every book published by Packt
- Copy-and-paste, print, and bookmark content
- On-demand and accessible via a web browser

Free access for Packt account holders

If you have an account with Packt at www.PacktPub.com, you can use this to access PacktLib today and view 9 entirely free books. Simply use your login credentials for immediate access.

Instant updates on new Packt books

Get notified! Find out when new books are published by following @PacktEnterprise on Twitter or the *Packt Enterprise* Facebook page.

*This book is dedicated to my dad, Dr K. M. Chhatrapati, with love.
Since my childhood, and even now, he always is my inspiration to be an activist
and a hardworker. I am sure he is proud of me in heaven.*

Table of Contents

Preface   **v**

Chapter 1: Team Foundation Server Primer   **1**

  Chapter objectives   **1**
  TFS basics   **2**
    Connecting the team   2
    Version control   3
    Planning the Agile process   3
    Processing build   4
    Maintaining test cases   5
    Reporting status   5
  ALM and TFS 2013   **6**
    ALM practices   6
    ALM with business trends   8
  The TFS 2013 architecture   **10**
    TFS on-premises   10
    Visual Studio Online   13
    Hybrid deployment   14
  TFS and reporting   **15**
    The reporting architecture   15
    Types of reports   17
  Summary   **18**

Chapter 2: Work Item Querying   **19**

  Team project scenario   **19**
  Work item queries   **20**
  Search box queries   **21**
  Flat queries   **22**
  Direct link queries   **29**

Tree queries   **32**
Summary   **34**
Chapter 3: Excel Reporting   **35**
Prerequisites to access Excel reports   **36**
Installing SharePoint Server Enterprise Edition   36
Provisioning a team project with a project portal   37
Integrating SharePoint 2013 with TFS 2013   38
    Mandatory permissions   38
Creating Excel reports   **39**
Creating Excel reports using a flat query list   39
Creating reports using Excel   41
Excel Project Management reports   **43**
The Burndown report   44
The Task Progress report   45
The User Story Progress report   46
The Issue Trends report   48
Bug Backlog Management Excel reports   **49**
The Bug Progress report   50
The Bug Trends report   52
The Bugs by Priority Report   53
The Bugs by Assignment report   54
The Bug Reactivations report   56
Build Management Excel reports   **58**
The Code Coverage report   59
The Code Churn report   60
The Build Status report   62
Test Management Excel reports   **63**
The Test Plan Progress report   64
The Test Case Readiness report   66
The User Story Test Status report   68
The Test Activity report   69
The Test Failure Analysis report   70
Summary   **72**
Chapter 4: SQL Server Reporting   **73**
SQL Server Reporting Services   **73**
SQL Server reporting tools   **74**
Report Builder   75
Report Designer   76

Understanding default SQL reports   **76**
Creating custom SQL reports   **80**
    Creating custom reports using Report Builder   81
    Creating custom reports using Report Designer   97
Summary   **112**

Chapter 5: Team Web Access Reporting   **113**
Granting an access level to a user or a group of users   **114**
    The basic access level   116
    The advanced access level   119
    The stakeholder access level   123
    Team web access charts   123
Team web access standard reports   **130**
    The velocity report   130
    The cumulative flow report   131
    The sprint burndown report   132
Summary   **133**
Index   **135**

Preface

This book is your guide to mastering the comprehensive reports that are part of Team Foundation Server and Microsoft's main Application Life Cycle Management (ALM) suite. TFS Reporting provides the ability to track different metrics of development projects throughout the Application Life Cycle; these include team progress, bugs, the current backlog, test progress, and so on, using well-integrated and familiar tools such as Excel and SQL Server Reporting Services. Team Web Access reports are also explained in this book, providing a quick progress status view via different charts, work item queries, as well as inbuilt reports. The book starts by giving you a walkthrough of TFS and the reporting architecture. Then it jumps into the basics of Excel reporting, describing each of the standard reports available. Finally, you will learn how to use the powerful tools available in SQL Server Reporting Services to create and customize robust reports and how to design and customize a dashboard featuring reports relevant to you.

What this book covers

Chapter 1, *Team Foundation Server Primer*, teaches the basics of the TFS architecture and reporting, and the importance of Application Life Cycle Management.

Chapter 2, *Work Item Querying*, explains the team project scenario in TFS walks through the types of work item query that results the required work items to know the status of work progress.

Chapter 3, *Excel Reporting*, explains the basics of integrating SharePoint 2013 with TFS 2013. This chapter also explores Excel report types and how to customize them as required need on different types of dashboards.

Chapter 4, SQL Server Reporting, walks through creating basic SQL reports using Report Builder and Report Designer.

Chapter 5, Team Web Access Reporting, explains Team Web Access levels and their various features (as required) and walks through a very light feature called work item charting. Also, it describes inbuilt standard reports.

What you need for this book

In order to understand the reporting functionalities for TFS 2013, you should have the following set up on the server:

- TFS 2013 to implement reports
- The sample Team project in TFS to base reports on
- SharePoint Server 2013, to integrate TFS with SharePoint for Excel reporting
- SQL Database 2012 or 2014 to store TFS and SharePoint databases
- Configuration of the Reporting and Analysis service in SQL Server for SQL reports

Who this book is for

This book is intended for developers, testers, architects, project managers, and for people who want to explore and make use of the reporting facilities of Team Foundation Server 2013 (TFS 2013). The primary audience is anyone working with software development at various cycles using TFS 2013 to administer the project team, source code, builds, work items, and test process. Although no previous experience of reporting is required, a basic understanding of Team Foundation components and project templates will be a plus.

Conventions

In this book, you will find a number of styles of text that distinguish between different kinds of information. Here are some examples of these styles, and an explanation of their meaning.

Code words in text, database table names, folder names, filenames, file extensions, pathnames, dummy URLs, user input, and Twitter handles are shown as follows: "At runtime, the `.rdlc` files are processed locally, while the `.rdl` files are processed remotely."

A block of code is set as follows:

```
SELECT   DimPerson.Name,
DimWorkItem.System_State,
DimWorkItem.System_Title
FROM     FactCurrentWorkItem INNER JOIN
```

New terms and **important words** are shown in bold. Words that you see on the screen, in menus or dialog boxes for example, appear in the text like this: "Clicking the **Next** button moves you to the next screen."

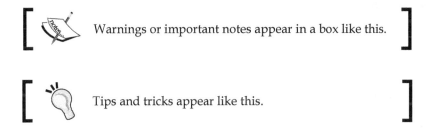

> Warnings or important notes appear in a box like this.

> Tips and tricks appear like this.

Reader feedback

Feedback from our readers is always welcome. Let us know what you think about this book—what you liked or may have disliked. Reader feedback is important for us to develop titles that you really get the most out of.

To send us general feedback, simply send an e-mail to feedback@packtpub.com, and mention the book title via the subject of your message.

If there is a topic that you have expertise in and you are interested in either writing or contributing to a book, see our author guide on www.packtpub.com/authors.

Customer support

Now that you are the proud owner of a Packt book, we have a number of things to help you to get the most from your purchase.

Downloading the color images of this book

We also provide you with a PDF file that has color images of the screenshots/diagrams used in this book. The color images will help you better understand the changes in the output. You can download this file from: https://www.packtpub.com/sites/default/files/downloads/6138EN_ColorImages.pdf

Errata

Although we have taken every care to ensure the accuracy of our content, mistakes do happen. If you find a mistake in one of our books—maybe a mistake in the text or the code—we would be grateful if you would report this to us. By doing so, you can save other readers from frustration and help us improve subsequent versions of this book. If you find any errata, please report them by visiting `http://www.packtpub.com/submit-errata`, selecting your book, clicking on the **errata submission form** link, and entering the details of your errata. Once your errata are verified, your submission will be accepted and the errata will be uploaded on our website, or added to any list of existing errata, under the Errata section of that title. Any existing errata can be viewed by selecting your title from `http://www.packtpub.com/support`.

Piracy

Piracy of copyright material on the Internet is an ongoing problem across all media. At Packt, we take the protection of our copyright and licenses very seriously. If you come across any illegal copies of our works, in any form, on the Internet, please provide us with the location address or website name immediately so that we can pursue a remedy.

Please contact us at `copyright@packtpub.com` with a link to the suspected pirated material.

We appreciate your help in protecting our authors, and our ability to bring you valuable content.

Questions

You can contact us at `questions@packtpub.com` if you are having a problem with any aspect of the book, and we will do our best to address it.

1
Team Foundation Server Primer

Team Foundation Server (**TFS**) is Microsoft's main tool to maintain development projects within the project team. It provides the collaborating platform for a software product. TFS also helps with maintaining source code with check-in/checkout and code review functionalities, building and testing the application, planning and tracking the work of team members, and so on. TFS is available as part of Microsoft's primary development suite, **Visual studio**. It is available on various Visual Studio editions such as Professional, Premium, Ultimate, and Test Professional. This chapter promotes a basic understanding of TFS, **Application Lifecycle Management** (**ALM**), and the TFS 2013 architecture.

Chapter objectives

This chapter covers the following topics:

- The basics of TFS
- ALM and TFS 2013
- The TFS 2013 architecture
- TFS 2013 and reporting

TFS basics

TFS is a set of tools and processes that are used to plan, develop, build, test, deploy, and maintain a software product. TFS forms the basis for Microsoft's Application Lifecycle Management (ALM) initiative. It also has a cloud version in **Azure** named **Visual Studio Online (VSO)**, which is known as **TFS Online** and has slightly different capabilities. VSO is a hub for project data on cloud, which can be up-and-running in a few minutes without installing and configuring a single server. We can connect to the project on cloud using the Visual Studio Development suite.

TFS ensures that the various software development methodologies and activities of an application include the following:

- Connecting the team
- Version Control
- Planning Agile Processes
- Maintaining test cases
- Reporting the status of the project

Connecting the team

The main purpose of TFS is to empower a team with easy-to-use methods and tools to develop software solutions. It enhances communication between team members, including developers, testers, the project manager, scrum master, and product owners, but also eases communication for external stakeholders by reporting all kinds of aspects within the development process such as bug reports, the results of testing, maintenance reports, work item reports, and so on. Everything in TFS is done within the context of a team project. The team project is used to maintain the project's development work where members are added and given access through which reports are generated and displayed. The following diagram indicates the connection between the project team and the TFS Server.

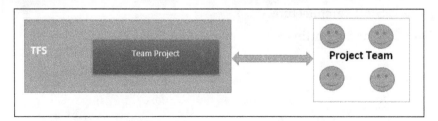

Version control

TFS provides version control to enable a team to manage and track the source files and documents in a project. It lets you to add not only code files but also documents, to maintain the project's documentation.

TFS version control has the following most useful activities:

- Check in/check out
- Managing versions
- Maintaining control of team projects
- Branching
- Shelving
- Defect tracking

Microsoft recommends using version control as early as possible in the project development life cycle. It helps to improve productivity and get rid of difficult problems.

 For more information on Version control, have a look at the following links:

- http://msdn.microsoft.com/en-us/library/ms181368.aspx
- http://msdn.microsoft.com/en-us/library/hh994655.aspx

Planning the Agile process

TFS supports agile methodologies by providing multiple process templates for agile projects and scrums. Third-party process templates can also be used to create your own template. Such templates help to plan, manage, and track a project team's work activities. The following are the main features provided by TFS for agile project development:

- Managing product backlogs
- Creating work items
- Breaking work items into tasks
- Assigning tasks to team members
- Tracking processes via a task board

In short, TFS provides real-time visibility with customizable boards while continuously monitoring the project status with flexible reporting. Agile tools are also available on Visual Studio Online.

> For more information on agile process planning, have a look at the following link:
>
> - `http://www.visualstudio.com/en-us/explore/agile-software-development-vs.aspx`
> - `http://msdn.microsoft.com/en-us/library/vstudio/ee889983.aspx`

Processing build

TFS allows continuous or periodic generation of project builds. A TFS build consists of the following activities:

- Synchronizing sources
- Compiling applications
- Running unit tests
- Performing code analysis
- Releasing builds on a file server
- Publishing build reports
- Scheduling a build
- Code check-in after build

In reality, TFS build server provides a way to define a build, which is then compiled and tested. Build systems help catch bugs and other quality issues during the development period and keep the code validated so that the application performs better.

> For more information on the build process, have a look at the following links:
>
> - `http://msdn.microsoft.com/en-us/library/vstudio/ms181709.aspx`
> - `http://msdn.microsoft.com/en-us/library/ms252495.aspx`

Maintaining test cases

The TFS family has a tool named Microsoft Test Management that is used to store test plans, create test cases, and run these test cases on a regular basis to increase the quality of the software product. It also helps find bugs encountered in an application. Generally, Microsoft Test Manager defines the test plan and manages the test cases for manual or automated tests. As we saw previously, test cases can be run during a build process; test cases are actually stored in a TFS server and closely integrated with every build process throughout the software product life cycle.

For more information on test case management, have a look at the following links:

- `http://msdn.microsoft.com/en-us/library/ms182409.aspx`
- `http://msdn.microsoft.com/en-us/library/jj635157.aspx`

Reporting status

Reporting is a basic segment in TFS that uses a separate data warehouse to generate the report. Tracking a team's work via reporting using work items, queries, builds, source code, and test results, is mainly used to represent graphical charts in a TFS report. Based on this report, we can make better decisions in order to drive the project seamlessly. There are a number of templates available to create reports. TFS can create custom reports as well. Every report depicts the status of the project, quality of the software, or progress of the project, which in turn results in better management of the software product throughout the team. We will discuss TFS reporting in more detail in later chapters

Ultimately, TFS is a focal point for the Application Life Cycle Management (ALM). It empowers the development team, project managers, and customers to effectively engage in the development process via a single solution.

ALM and TFS 2013

Application Life cycle Management (ALM) manages a project's life cycle in order to improve efficiency and reduce risk. It's basically a strategy that describes how to develop the code and work together. Application Lifecycle Management (ALM) is a set of proven practices that are used to manage the development process of the project that can be achieved via the Visual Studio development suite. These are the specific tools that are used to understand the customer's needs, and hence the team can effectively design, implement, and deploy the code.

> Wikipedia Definition: Application lifecycle management (ALM) is the product lifecycle management (governance, development, and maintenance) of application software. It encompasses requirements management, software architecture, computer programming, software testing, software maintenance, change management, project management, and release management.

ALM practices

ALM's core practices are as follow:

- Building the TFS Environment setup
- Creating a team project in TFS
- Adding team member accounts in a team project
- Sharing the code using version control in TFS
- Planning project work items
- Tracking the team's work
- Generating reports
- Setting up a build server
- Defining build processes
- Testing an application

The latest features of TFS 2013 and VSO empower team members to develop and manage the project that result in the best experience across the platforms. Moreover, additional ALM features help team members become more productive with improved support of agile software development practices. Most businesses require flawless synchronization of data across different ALM tools/solutions without losing focus on the value of a corporate ALM strategy.

Visual Studio Online (VSO) is also an ALM tool hosted in the cloud that has all the features of an on-premise TFS, minus the administration headache associated with an on-premise version.

Visual Studio Online (VSO) is a set of essential components on a cloud-based service to write better code. It offers code browsing, code editing, repository places to check-in /check out your code, build services, test case management, and application insights.

Using Visual Studio Online (VSO), you can create team projects, choose a process template that suits your project, and perform all the workflows associated with Sprint Planning and Project Management using the Agile methodology. The core capability of TFS 2013 is ALM, which has been evolving through various practices, tools, and processes, as depicted in the following:

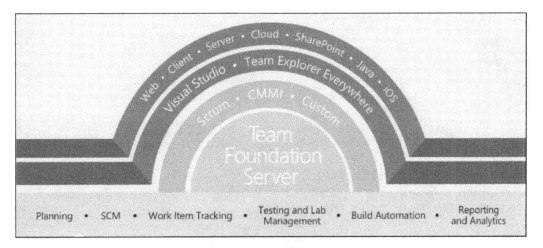

TFS 2013 is the first requirement in setting up the environment in order to follow Application Lifecycle Management (ALM) practices and tools. It's designed to integrate all artifacts across the software development life cycle. It simply includes managing the source control and tracking work items that can be everything from requirements to bugs. All these things can be wrapped using process templates such as **Scrum**, **CMMI**, or custom ones, as required.

ALM with business trends

These days, business requirements have been changing to implement the business application from a single server to a hybrid server or completely on-cloud across various devices. The following screenshot represents some of the latest business trends that can be fulfilled via the Application Lifecycle Management (ALM) process:

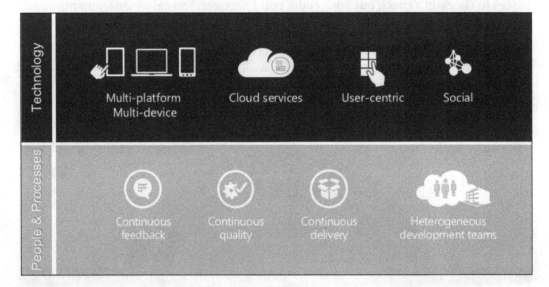

By considering the latest business trends, ALM focuses more on building the application, measuring the application, and learning the application; this is called as the **BUILD-MEASURE-LEARN** cycle.

As we develop software, we get continuous feedback that goes to the project team and supplies insight into improving the project. Along with this, ALM can be broken down in to four major areas: plan, develop, release, and operate, that *continuously adds value* to the solution, as shown in the following screenshot:

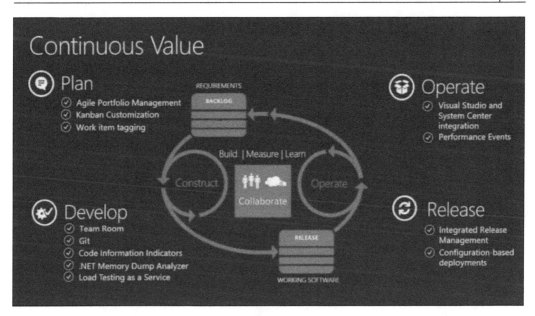

The current business scenario indicates that delivering high-quality, modern applications requires modern application lifecycle management (ALM) tools and processes. ALM offers processes and tools to enable software development teams to be more productive and collaborate more effectively with all project team members.

For more information on Application Lifecycle Management (ALM), have a look at the following links:

- `http://msdn.microsoft.com/en-us/library/vstudio/fda2bad5(v=vs.120).aspx`
- `http://channel9.msdn.com/Events/TechEd/Australia/2013/DEV211`
- `http://msdn.microsoft.com/en-s/library/vstudio/ee889983.aspx`

The TFS 2013 architecture

TFS 2013 is built on multilevel scalable architecture. To set up the TFS environment for the project team, it's very important to figure out the architecture of TFS in order to understand the business need deployment strategy.

TFS can be deployed in three ways:

- On-premises with a single server or multiple servers across one domain or workgroup or domains
- On-cloud, where all deployments are server-hosted by Microsoft
- Hybrid Deployment, with TFS features as well as Visual Studio Online (VSO)

Based on business requirements, TFS architecture topology can be decided by considering the following:

- The Application, Data, and Client tiers
- The location of servers
- TFS Build computers and their locations
- Their necessity for a TFS server proxy
- Ensuring client access for the service on port 443
- Web services, databases, and object models
- Default TFS ports and protocols
- Permissions on TFS components

TFS on-premises

With TFS on-premises, we can extend the features and functionalities of the Team Foundation by writing the application either on the client side or on the application server. The TFS architecture is mainly divided into 4 parts:

- Client side: By using a client object model, we can extend TFS capabilities that relate to version control, tracking work items, and building on the client side.

- Application tier: By using a server object model, we can extend TFS functionalities on an application tier that relate to integrating other tools and data into TFS.

- Data tier: This includes data, stored procedures, and other associated logic. The data tier consists of the following databases within a SQL server:

  ° Configuration database

  ° Application warehouse

  ° Analysis service database

  ° Team project collection database

- Build machine: We can customize the build process using the build process object model on a build machine that relates to creating build processes and activities, as shown in the following TFS Architecture diagram:

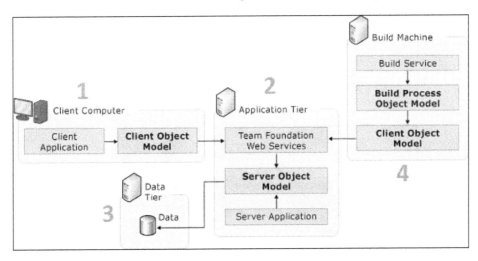

For instance, TFS server hosts multiple team projects and each project will have a repository that will have four branches such as Development, **System Integration Testing (SIT)**, **User Acceptance Test (UAT)**, and Production, as shown in the following team project hierarchy:

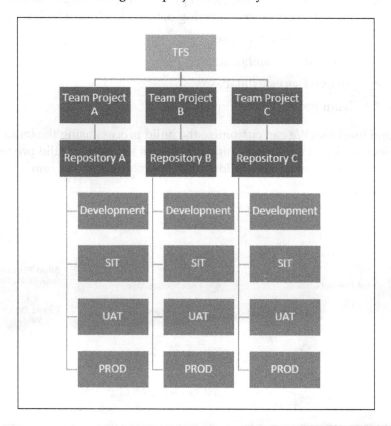

The code in the repositories resides in the data tier, which is accessible using a client application stored on the client side through the application tier. For each branch, you can configure one or more multiple build processes. These builds requires a build server. We can have one build server for all the builds or a separate build server for each repository; alternatively, it can be share a build server between two repositories.

Visual Studio Online

Microsoft also came up with the choice of using Visual Studio Online (VSO), which facilitates all server-side deployments. For example, all source code, work items, build configuration, and team features are hosted on-cloud by Microsoft. This feature immensely simplifies deployment, as we only need to bother with client-side components and Internet access.

In order to access cloud-based TFS, we require a Microsoft account to connect to the service on-cloud using a web browser. Using Visual Studio Online (VSO), we can perform activities such as creating team projects, adding members to the team, and working as you wish, as you do for locally deployed TFS; this is like getting rid of the administering servers. The following screenshot shows the flow of Visual Studio Online (VSO) and Team Project:

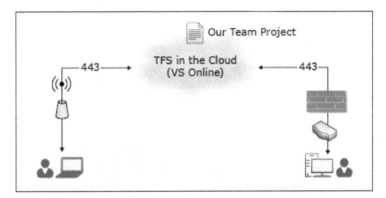

In Visual Studio Online (VSO) deployment, the application tier, data tier, and build server are hosted on the cloud via the Microsoft Cloud platform and SQL server Azure technology.

Hybrid deployment

However, there are still arguments for having TFS on-premise and Visual Studio Online (VSO). The following points are the main differences between TFS on-premises and TFS on-cloud:

Feature	TFS on-premise	TFS on-cloud (VSO)
Customized work items and process templates	√	X
SharePoint and Project server Integration	√	X
Data warehousing and Reporting service	√	X
CodeLense Support	√	X
Active Directory Support	√	X
Data availability within the network	√	X
Application Insights	X	√
Cloud Load Testing	X	√
Always on the latest version	X	√
Simple installation	X	√
Virtual Team Rooms	X	√
Supports Microsoft IDs	X	√

Team Foundation Server has customizable work items and process templates, enterprise-level reporting, and incredible scalability. Visual Studio Online (VSO) has elastic load testing, Application Insights, and deep integration with Azure. It looks as if enterprises have to choose one or the other, but it's not always true. We can have the advantage of both to add more power to Application Life Cycle Management.

There are various integration tools available for TFS and Visual Studio Online (VSO). All are open source and you can choose one as per your requirements; they are as follows:

- Code Plex Integration Tools
- Team Foundation Server Integration Tools
- ALM Rangers

For more information on the TFS 2013 architecture, have a look at the following links:

- `http://channel9.msdn.com/Events/TechEd/NorthAmerica/2014/DEV-B363#fbid=`
- `http://visualstudiogallery.msdn.microsoft.com/eb77e739-c98c-4e36-9ead-fa115b27fefe`

TFS and reporting

TFS 2013 has a reporting service that you can use to design reports; you can display them on the dashboard in order to show the team's progress in the project's development life cycle. As this book's main focus is on TFS reporting, it's important to understand how data flows in TFS for the reporting service and its architecture.

The reporting architecture

The reporting service is integrated with a SQL server as it has a separate data warehouse to generate reports. The main component of the **TFS reporting architecture** are:

- **Operational Stores**: Every activity in TFS gets stored in relational databases in the SQL server, these are known as **operational stores**. These mainly contain the TFS configuration and team project collection information.

- **Warehouse adapters**: These are manageable assemblies that fetch data from operational stores and transform them into a standardized format that is compatible with warehouse databases and writes them to the warehouse relational databases.

- **Relational Databases**: These have a schema that specifies the fields such as dimensions, measures, and reporting data details. The data warehouse is organized in a star schema, consisting of fact tables and dimension tables. For example, the `work item fact` table has one row for every work item stored in the work item operational store. Fact tables are a good source of information for the reports and show the latest activity. A dimension table stores the set of values that exists for given dimensions. Measures are the values taken from operational data.

- **Analysis service cube**: To report about day-to-day work items or test results, the warehouse needs to retain the state of every item for each day; this allows the data cube to aggregate the measures by day. The data cube aggregates the data from the relational databases. Whenever the data cube is processed, the data from the relational databases is pulled into the cube to get aggregated and stored. The cube provides a central place to obtain data for reports without having to know the schema for each operational store and access each store separately.

- **Reporting with Report Designer**: This is a tool in Visual Studio that is used to design the reports. Report Designer provides tabbed windows for data, layout and preview, query builder, and an expression editor to create a report.

- **Excel Reports**: TFS is integrated with Excel to manage projects and its reports that use Microsoft Excel. Microsoft Excel provides pivot tables and charts to view and analyze multidimensional data. You can bind these pivot tables directly to the Team Foundation cube, so you can interact with the data in the cube.

- **Security**: TFS administers have access to the data in the data warehouse by granting or revoking permissions on the user's account. By default, write access to the warehouse is restricted to a service account under which the warehouse service runs. A user who has permission to view the data in the warehouse has full access to all of the data for all team projects in all team project collections.

The following diagram shows the reporting architecture for TFS 2013:

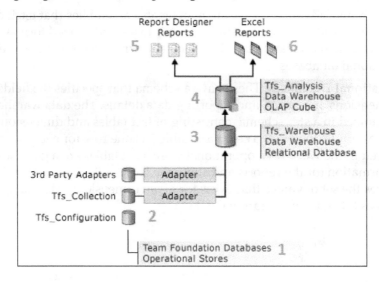

For more information on TFS and Reporting, have a look at the following links:

- `http://msdn.microsoft.com/en-us/library/ff647430.aspx`
- `http://msdn.microsoft.com/en-us/library/bb649552.aspx`
- `http://msdn.microsoft.com/en-us/library/ms244687.aspx`
- `http://blogs.msdn.com/b/jasonsingh/archive/2013/03/27/tfs-reports-alm-means-the-everyone-from-your-vp-to-your-customer.aspx`

Types of reports

TFS 2013 offers the following types of report, which we will look at in depth in later chapters:

- **Work item queries**: These are used to review or update work items.

- **Work item reporting**: Custom work item reports are generated using Microsoft Excel, the project server, and SSRS reporting tools.

- **Excel reports**: There are a number of standard Excel reports available via the selected process template while creating a team project; these reports can be accessed via the SharePoint portal or Team Explorer's **Document** tab.

- **SSRS reports**: There are a number of default reports available via the selected process template with installed SSRS; these can be accessed via Web Access, SharePoint or Team Explorer.

- **Team Web Access reports**: TFS 2013 has excellent chart and standard reports that show a visual representation of work items. It can be accessed via Team Web Access.

- **Light weight reports**: TFS 2013 introduced a new feature called **light weight reporting** that provides the ability to create real-time reports based on query results and does not rely on the warehouse or cube. It offers real-time Burndown charts, velocity, and CFD diagrams directly within Team Web access.

- **SQL queries**: Major reports in TFS display information from the analysis service OLAP cube. However, running T-SQL queries directly against relational databases provides the facility to create more granular-level custom reports.

- **TFS API**: This provides binaries to create a custom report using only a few lines of C# code.

- **REST API**: Currently, this API is only available in Visual Studio Online (VSO) and is an implementation of OData Protocol. The REST API makes it dramatically easier to integrate Visual Studio Online (VSO) with other web-based tools and to access VS Online from any mobile device, irrespective of whether they are third-party commercial tools or custom ones you are building.

Summary

In this chapter, we reviewed the basics of TFS Architecture and Reporting. We also reviewed the importance of Application Life Cycle Management. In the next chapter, we will emphasize on creating work item reports from queries.

2
Work Item Querying

Work items are the primary element project managers and team leaders focus on to track and identify the pending work to be completed. A team member uses work items to track their personal work queue. In order to achieve the current status of the project via work items, it's essential to query work items based on the requirements.

This chapter will cover the following topics:

- Team project scenario
- Work item queries
- Search box queries
- Flat queries
- Direct link queries
- Tree queries

Team project scenario

Here, we are considering a sports item website that helps user to buy sport items from an item gallery based on their category. The user has to register for membership in order to buy sport products such as footballs, tennis rackets, cricket bats, and so on. Moreover, a registered user can also view/add sport-related articles or news, which will be visible to everyone irrespective of whether they are anonymous or registered. This project is mapped with TFS and has a repository created in TFS Server with work items such as user stories, tasks, bugs, and test cases to plan and track the project's work.

We have the following TFS configuration settings for the team project:

- Team Foundation Server: **DIPSTFS**
- Website project: **SportsWeb**
- Team project: **SportsWebTeamProject**
- Team Foundation Server URL: `http://dipstfs:8080/tfs`
- Team project collection URL: `http://dipstfs:8080/tfs/DefaultCollection`
- Team Project URL: `http://dipstfs:8080/tfs/DefaultCollection/SportsWebTeamProject`
- Team project administrators: `DIPSTFS\DipsAdministrator`
- Team project members: `DIPSTFS\Dipti Chhatrapati, DIPSTFS\Bjoern H Rapp, DIPSTFS\Edric Taylor, DIPSTFS\John Smith, DIPSTFS\Nelson Hall, DIPSTFS\Scott Harley`

The following figure shows the project with TFS configuration and setup:

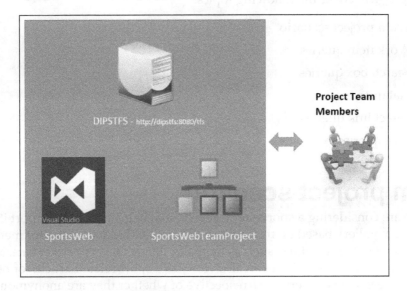

Work item queries

Work item queries smoothen the process of identifying the status of the team project; this helps in creating a custom report in TFS. We can query work items by a search box or a query editor via Team Web Access.

For more information on Work Item Queries, have a look at following links:

- http://msdn.microsoft.com/en-us/library/ms181308(v=vs.110).aspx
- http://msdn.microsoft.com/en-us/library/dd286638.aspx

There are three types of queries:

- Flat queries
- Direct link queries
- Tree queries

Search box queries

We can find a work item using the search box available in the team project web portal, which is shown in the following screenshot:

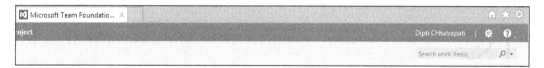

You can type in keywords in the search box located on top right of the team project web portal site; for example **master**, will result in the following work items:

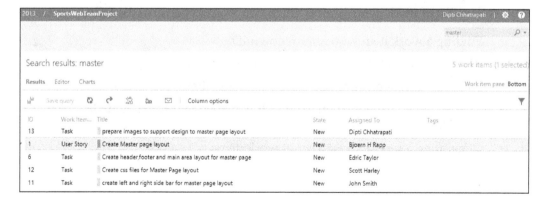

The search box content menu also has the ability to find work items based on assignment, status, created by, or work item type, as shown in the following screenshot:

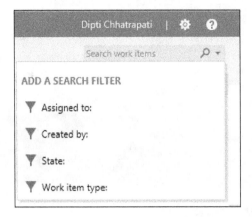

The search box finds items using shortcut filters or by specifying keywords or phrases, specific fields/field values, assignment or date modifications, or using the equals, contains, and not operators.

 For more information on search box filtering, have a look at `http://msdn.microsoft.com/en-us/library/cc668120.aspx`.

Flat queries

A flat query list of work items is used when you want to perform the following tasks:

- Finding a work item with an unknown ID
- Checking the status or other columns of work items
- Finding work items that you want to link to other work items
- Exporting work items to Microsoft Office, Microsoft Excel, and Office Project for bulk updates to column fields
- Generating a report about a set of work items

As a general practice, to easily find work items, a team member can create **Shared Queries**, which are predefined queries shared across the team. They can be created, modified, and saved as a new query too.

The following steps demonstrate how to open a flat query list and create a new query list:

1. In the team project web portal, expand **Shared Query List** located on the left-hand side and click on the **My Tasks** query, as shown in the following screenshot:

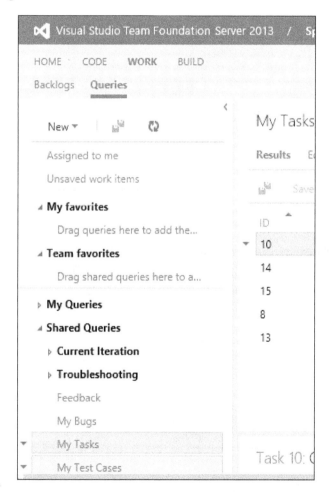

2. The resulting work items generated by the **My Tasks** query will be shown in the **Work item pane**, as shown in the following screenshot:

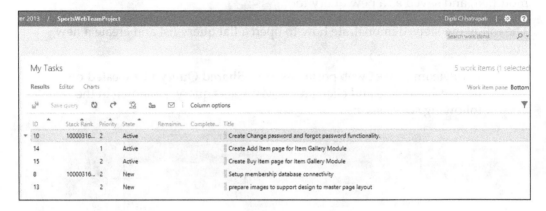

3. As there are now three active tasks and two new tasks, we will create the **My Active Tasks** flat Query. To do so, click on **Editor**, as shown here:

4. Add a clause to filter work items by **Active State**:

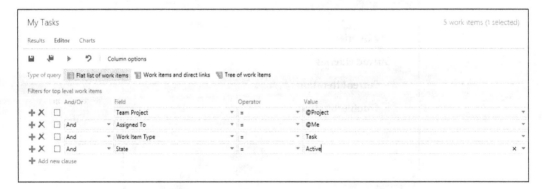

5. Now click on the **Save Query as...** icon to save the query as **My Active Task**:

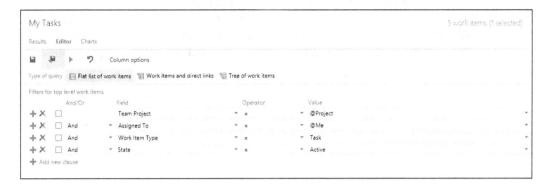

6. Enter the query name and folder as appropriate. Here, we will save the query in the **Shared Queries** Folder and click on **OK**:

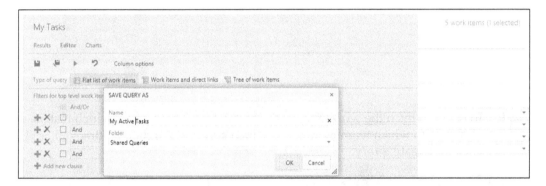

7. Click on **Results** to view the work items for the **My Active Tasks** query and it will display the items, as shown in the following screenshot:

8. Now let's have a look at how to create a query that represents all the work item details of different sprints/iterations. For example, you have a number of sprints in the **Release 1** iteration and another release to test an application that's named **Test Release 1** that you can find in Team Web Access site's settings page under the **Iterations** tab, as indicated in the following screenshot:

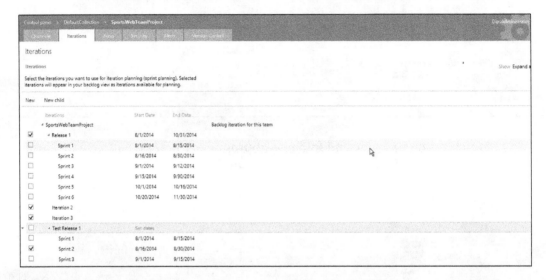

9. In order to fetch the work item data of all the sprints to know which task is allocated to which team member in which sprint, go to the **Backlogs** tab and click on **Create query**:

10. Specify the query name and folder location to store the query. Then click on **OK**:

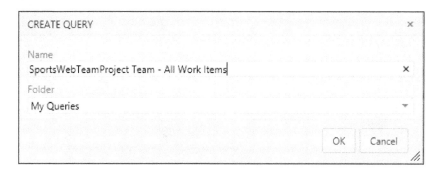

11. Then click on the link as indicated in the following screenshot, which will redirect you to the created query:

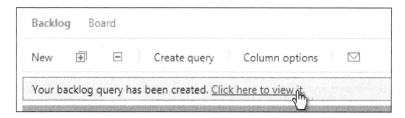

12. Click on **Flat list of work items** and remove all the conditions except the iteration path, as shown in the following screenshot:

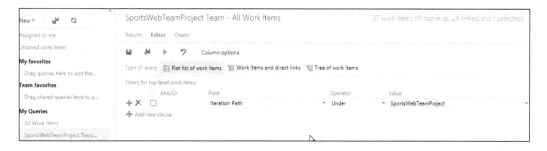

13. Now save the query and run it. Add columns such as **Work Item Type,
    State**, **Iteration Path**, **Title**, and **Assigned To** as appropriate. As a result,
    this query will display the work items available under the team project for
    different sprints or releases, as indicated in the following screenshot:

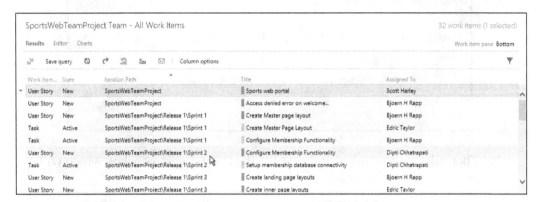

14. To filter work items based on the sprint\release\iteration, change
    the iteration path condition for **Value** to **Sprint 1**, as indicated in the
    following screenshot:

15. Finally, save and run the query, which will return the work items available under **Sprint 1** of the **Release 1** iteration:

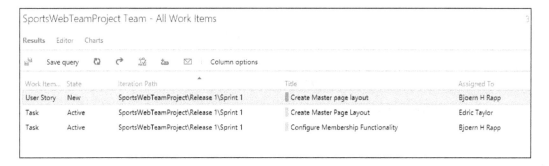

 For more information on flat queries, have a look at `http://msdn.microsoft.com/en-us/library/ms181308(v=vs.110).aspx`.

Direct link queries

There are work items that are dependent on other work items such as tasks, bugs, and issues, and they can be tracked using direct links. They help determine risks and dependencies in order to collaborate among teams effectively.

Direct link queries help perform the following tasks:

- Creating a custom view of linked work items
- Tracking dependencies across team projects and manage the commitments made to other project teams
- Assesing changes to work items that you do not own but that your work items depend on

The following steps demonstrate how to generate a linked query list:

1. Open **My Tasks List** from **Shared Queries**.
2. Click on **Editor**.

3. Click on **Work items and direct links,** as shown in the following screenshot:

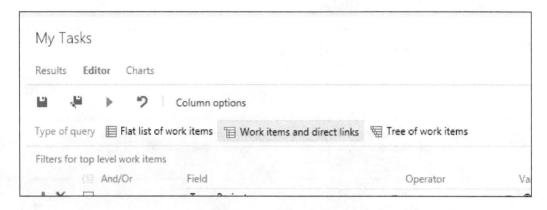

4. Specify the clause for the work item type: **Task** in **Filters for linked work items:**

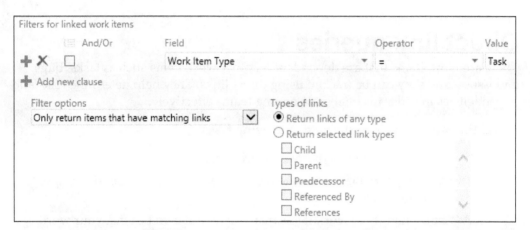

5. We can filter the first level work items by choosing the following option:

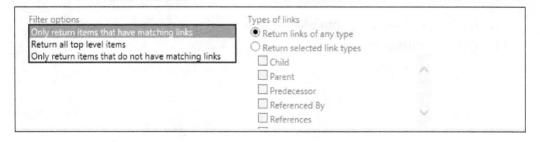

The meanings of the filter options are described as follows:

- ○ **Only return work items that have the specified links**: This option returns only the top-level work items that have links to work items.

- ○ **Return all top level work items**: This option returns all the work items whether they have linked work items or not. This option also returns the second-level work items that are linked to the first-level work items.

- ○ **Only return work items that do not have the specified links**: This option returns only the top-level work items those are not linked to any work items.

6. Run the query, save it as **My Linked Tasks** and click on **OK**:

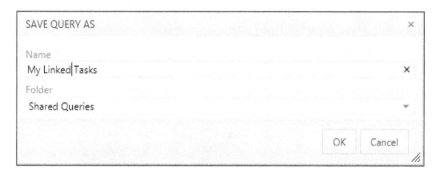

7. Click on **Results** to view the linked tasks as configured previously.

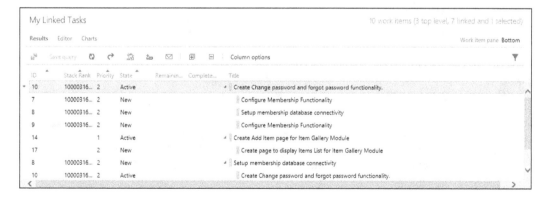

 For more information on direct link queries, have a look at http://msdn.microsoft.com/en-us/library/ dd286501(v=vs.110).aspx.

Tree queries

To view nested work items, tree queries are used by selecting the **Tree of Work Items** query type.

Tree queries are used to execute following tasks:

- Viewing the hierarchy
- Finding parent or child work items
- Changing the tree hierarchy
- Exporting the tree view to Microsoft Excel for either bulk updates to column fields or to change the tree hierarchy

The following steps demonstrate how to generate a tree query list:

1. Open the **My Tasks** list from **Shared Queries**.
2. Click on **Editor**.
3. Click on **Tree of work items**, as shown in the following screenshot:

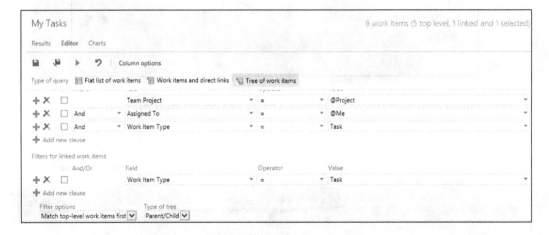

 Define the filter criteria for both parent and child work items. Specify the clause for work item type: **Task** in **Filters for linked work items**. Also, select **Match top-level work items first**.

4. We can filter linked work items by choosing the following option:

To find linked children, select **Match top-level work items first** and, to find linked parents, select **Match linked work items first**.

5. Run the query, save it as **My Tree Tasks**, and click on **OK**.

6. Click on **Results** to view the linked tasks as configured previously:

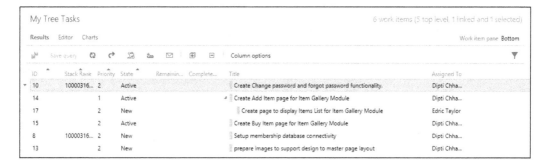

 For more information on Tree queries, have a look at: http://msdn. microsoft.com/en-us/library/dd286633(v=vs.110).aspx

Summary

In this chapter, we reviewed the team project scenario that will be featured throughout the book to understand reporting functions. We also walked through the types of work item queries that produce work items we need in order to know the status of work progress.

In the next chapter, you will learn about Excel reporting to generate a work items report in an Excel sheet in the form of charts and tables.

3
Excel Reporting

Excel Reporting in TFS helps create effective queries and reports to manage the team project impressively. Microsoft Excel connects with TFS Data Warehouse and displays the data from TFS Data Warehouse on a **PivotTable** or **PivotChart**. The project teams can quickly get necessary information about their respective team projects using various reporting dashboards. **Dashboards** display project data, support investigations, and help the team work on common tasks more swiftly.

In this chapter, we will learn about the following topics:

- Prerequisites to access Excel reports
- Excel report creation
- Excel Management reports
- Bug Backlog Management Excel reports
- Build Management Excel reports
- Test Management Excel reports

Prerequisites to access Excel reports

In this section, we will discuss the configurations required for TFS in order to execute and view Excel reports.

Installing SharePoint Server Enterprise Edition

To enable Excel reports, the team project needs to be configured with the SharePoint site created using the SharePoint Server Enterprise edition. TFS facilitates the use of dashboards, such as Burndown, Quality, Bug, Test, and Build, that display the team project's reporting data via different types of Excel reports. This helps find relevant information about the team project's progress easily. We will talk about the Excel reports used in each of the dashboards later.

You can see all the available dashboards on the SharePoint site, as follows:

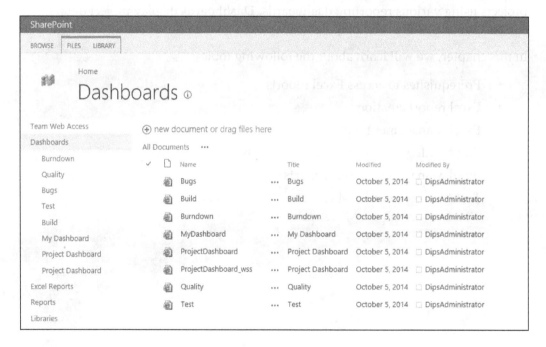

The following are the dashboards that you will see in the **Dashboards** section:

- **Burndown Dashboard**: Also known as the Progress Dashboard, this contains Excel reports that are used to track the team project's progress with respect to completing the iteration
- **Quality Dashboard**: This contains Excel reports that are used to get an overview of progress on the development, test, and build areas so as to identify the quality of the team project
- **Bugs Dashboard**: This contains Excel reports that are used to monitor the bug activity of the team project
- **Test Dashboard**: This contains Excel reports that help in finding gaps in test coverage and test activities, and identifying test areas that might require additional investigation and then report their progress
- **Build Dashboard**: This contains Excel reports that give an overview of the development activities that affect the quality of the builds
- **My Dashboard**: This contains Excel reports that help view tasks or work items assigned to each team member
- **Project Dashboard**: This contains Excel reports that track the team's progress towards completing the iteration or sprint work

> For more information about SharePoint's configuration with TFS and different types of dashboards, have a look at the following links:
>
> - http://msdn.microsoft.com/en-us/library/dd578615.aspx
> - http://msdn.microsoft.com/en-us/library/hh667648.aspx
> - https://msdn.microsoft.com/en-us/library/dd380719.aspx

Provisioning a team project with a project portal

To use Excel reports, a team project must be provisioned with a team project portal. Excel reports are stored on SharePoint Server via the SharePoint site. If the project portal is not enabled for the team project, accessing the workbook is impossible. The team project portal site is linked with the team project in order to share information. Thus, the project portal is important to enable access to shared documents and dashboards for Excel reports.

For more information about provisioning team projects in TFS, go to https://msdn.microsoft.com/en-us/library/ms242865.aspx.

Integrating SharePoint 2013 with TFS 2013

Once SharePoint has been installed in the same domain where TFS exists, the next step is to configure SharePoint with TFS. This requires configuring the following for the TFS server:

- Installing extensions for SharePoint products
- Configuring the SharePoint web application
- Configuring SharePoint sites

 For more information about configuring TFS to use SharePoint, go to https://msdn.microsoft.com/en-us/library/dd631915.aspx.

Mandatory permissions

Team members must have the following permissions on the SharePoint site that is linked with the team project:

- Read permissions to view the reporting dashboards
- Contribute permissions to edit and copy the dashboard

To customize the report in Microsoft Office Excel, a team member must be a member of the tfswarehousedatareaders security role in SQL Server Analysis Services and contribute permissions on the SharePoint site that is linked with the team project.

Also, to operate work items, the following permissions are required:

- **Read permission**: This helps view a work item that can be configured by adding team members in the readers group of the team project portal. Another option is to ensure the View work items in this node permission are set to allow team members.
- **Contribute permission**: This helps create or modify a work item and can be configured by adding team members in the Contributors group of the team project portal. Another option is that editing work items in this node permission must be allowed for team members.

For more information about permissions in TFS, go to:
`https://msdn.microsoft.com/en-us/library/bb649553.aspx`

It is recommended that you configure the SharePoint web application for Single Sign-on if the team project portal is configured to use **NT LAN Manager** (**NTLM**) authentication.

Creating Excel reports

Creating Excel reports using work item queries is one of the easiest ways to generate custom reports. Excel reports via a work item query let you generate status and trend graphs. Once the reports are generated, data can be manipulated by adding or filtering the fields using a PivotTable.

Creating Excel reports using a flat query list

The following diagram shows the item count per member generated by a flat query list:

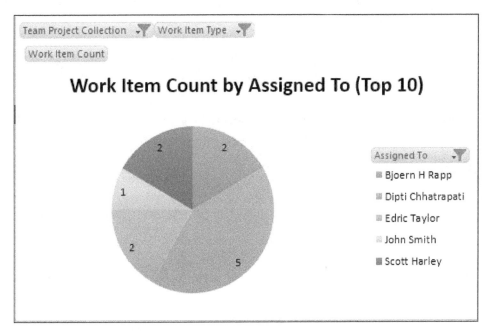

The following are the steps to generate Excel reports using a flat query list:

1. Open the flat query list, in Team Explorer in Visual Studio, that contains the items to be reported. For example, the **All Tasks shared** query considers all work items to have the task type as displayed in the following screenshot:

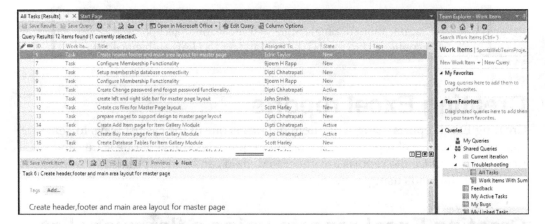

2. Create a report in Microsoft Excel from the query results view:

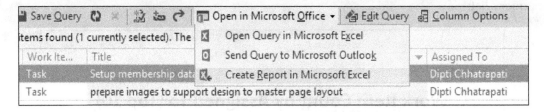

3. Select the desired details for the report to be generated.

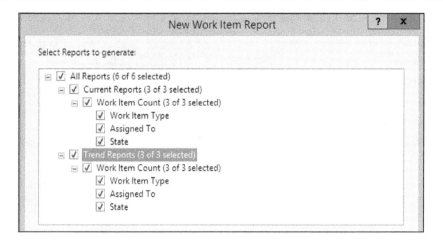

4. Click on **Finish** and wait until Excel completes the report generation process.

5. As a result, Excel reports, in which every worksheet shows the report, have been generated. These reports have pie charts displaying status reports as well as area graphs displaying trend charts.

6. To view the report, select a worksheet. For example, click on **Assigned To** to view the work item count per team member, as shown in the earlier screenshot.

Creating reports using Excel

There are also ways to generate query-based reports using Excel, as shown in the following steps:

1. Open an Microsoft Excel Office workbook and select **New Report** from the **Team** tab.

2. Connect to the TFS server.

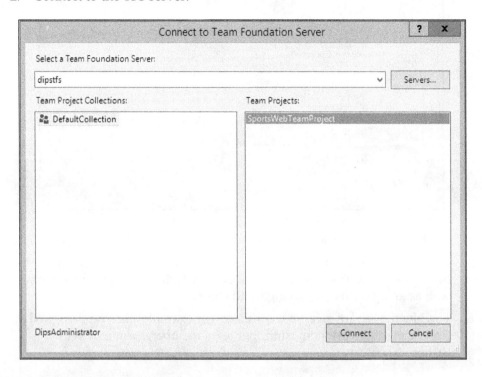

3. Select the desired query, for example, **All Tasks**, and click on **Next**.

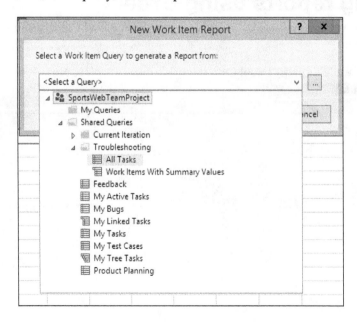

4. Repeat steps 3 to 6 from the *Creating Excel report using a flat query list* section to generate the report.

Excel Project Management reports

In most project development teams, the following reports are frequently used to estimate the team's progress against completing tasks, finishing user stories, and achieving the iteration plan. These reports are available on the Burndown dashboard on the SharePoint site, that is associated with the team project portal. The Burndown dashboard shows four Excel reports that help monitor progress, Burndown, and other issues. These reports are as follows:

- The Burndown Excel report
- The Task Progress report
- The User Story Progress Excel report
- The Issue Trends Excel report

In order to have accurate data on the Burndown dashboard for the preceding Excel reports, team members need to perform the following activities on TFS:

- Defining user stories from the product backlog
- Specifying the area and iteration paths for each user's story item
- Updating the state of each user's story item
- Defining tasks
- Specifying the area and iteration paths for each task item
- Updating the completed and remaining hours for each task item
- Updating the state (active/closed) for each task item
- Defining issues
- Updating the state (active/closed) for each issue item

 If a task has been divided into subtasks, then each team member has to specify hours only for the subtasks. These hours are rolled up as summary values for the parent task and user story.

Let's discuss the reports that are useful for monitoring the team work activity of the project.

The Burndown report

The **Burndown** report is used to determine the team's progress towards work completion. The following are the characteristics of the **Burndown** report:

- **Chart description**: The **Burndown** chart is a graphical display of the aggregated count of all of the hours for all the tasks implemented in the last four weeks. The following chart represents the completed work and remaining work hours for completed iterations:

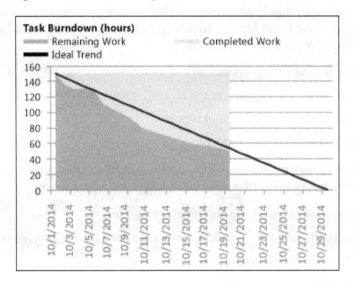

In the preceding graph, the *x* axis indicates planned days of the four weeks, and the *y* axis indicates the planned 150 hours. An inclined black line represents the ideal team progress. This line is drawn from the *y* axis showing the remaining work hours on the start date, to the *x* axis on the end date.

- **Analysis**: This report helps determine the following aspects of work progress during the iteration in the team:

  - The speed of the project development team's work

  - The estimate of the remaining work in the available hours

  - The final end time for the remaining work

  - Seeing whether the project can be completed at the end of the iteration

- **Update and customization**: To update and customize the Burndown report, open the Excel report file named **Burndown** in edit mode from the SharePoint document library named **Excel Reports**. By changing the following filter options of the PivotTable, the report gets customized as per your need:

  ◦ To view Burndown for iteration, edit the **Work Item Iteration Hierarchy** filter option, which is selected by default as **All**.

  ◦ To view Burndown for a product area, edit the **Work Item Area Hierarchy** filter option, which is selected by default as **All**.

  ◦ To view Burndown for a specific interval, edit the **Date** file. Specify the start date and drag the fill till the end date. After changing the date range, click on **Refresh All** from the **Data** tab.

The Task Progress report

The **Task Progress** report is used to trace the amount of work the team has accomplished and the amount of work that remains. The following are the characteristics of the **Task Progress** report:

- **Chart description**: The **Task Progress** report is a visual illustration of the aggregate count of all the active and closed tasks implemented in the last four weeks. This chart represents the share of active and closed tasks of iteration, as indicated in the following screenshot:

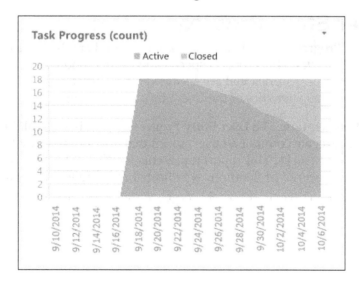

In the preceding graph, the *x*-axis indicates days from the past four weeks, and the *y*-axis indicates the work item count.

- **Analysis**: This report helps determine the following aspects of Task Progress during the iteration in the team:

  - Team progress towards finishing tasks
  - Team work additions

- **Update and customization**: To update and customize the Task Progress report, open the Excel report file named **Task Progress** in edit mode from the SharePoint document library named **Excel Reports**. By changing the following filter options of the PivotTable, the report gets customized in line with your requirements:

  - To view the **Task Progress** graph for the tasks throughout the iteration, edit the **Work Item Iteration Hierarchy** filter option, which is selected by default as **All**

  - To view the **Task Progress** graph of the tasks for a product area, edit the **Work Item Area Hierarchy** filter option, which is selected by default as **All**

  - To view the **Task Progress** graph for the tasks for a specific interval, edit the **Rows/Columns** field from **PivotTable Field List** by specifying a particular set of weeks

The User Story Progress report

The **User Story Progress** report is used to trace the speed at which the team is working on user stories. This report is specifically used to know how close the team is to finishing their user stories that are specified for an iteration or release. The following are the characteristics of the User Story Progress report:

- **Chart description**: The **User Story Progress** report is a visual illustration of the aggregate count of all user stories that are organized by their state in the last four weeks. This report represents the share of active, resolved, and closed user stories of iteration, as indicated in the following figure:

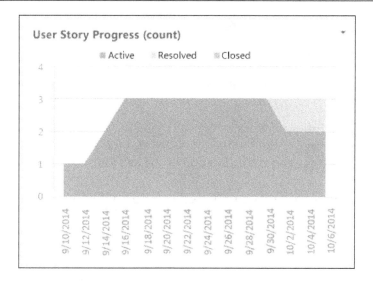

In the preceding graph, the x axis indicates the past four weeks' days and the y axis indicates the user story count.

- **Analysis**: This report helps determine the following aspects of a user story's progress during the iteration in the team:
    - Team progress during iteration or release
    - Team progress with respect to closing or resolving tasks

- **Update and customization**: To update and customize the **User Story Progress** report, open the Excel report file named **User Story Progress** in edit mode from the SharePoint document library named **Excel Reports**. By changing the following filter options for the PivotTable, the report gets customized in line with your requirements:
    - To view the **User Story Progress** graph of the tasks throughout the iteration, edit the **Work Item Iteration Hierarchy** filter option, which is selected by default as **All**
    - To view the **User Story Progress** graph of the tasks for a product area, edit the **Work Item Area Hierarchy** filter option, which is selected by default as **All**
    - To view the **User Story Progress** graph for the tasks for a specific interval, edit the **Rows/Columns** field from the PivotTable Field List by specifying a particular set of weeks

The Issue Trends report

The **Issue Trends** report is used to trace the rate at which the team is receiving and fixing issues. This report is specifically used to figure out the number of issues that the team is facing currently. The following are the characteristics of the Issue Trends report:

- **Chart description**: The **Issue Trends** report is a line chart that represents the running average of the number of issues that the team has opened, resolved, and closed throughout the iteration of the last four weeks, as indicated in the following screenshot:

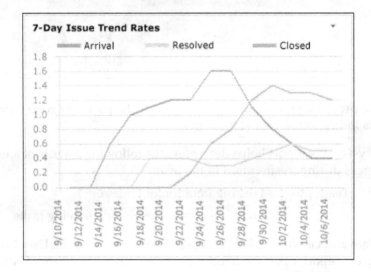

In the preceding graph, the *x* axis indicates days of the last four weeks, and the *y* axis indicates the running average that is based on the report seven days prior to the date for which it is computed. In other words, the graph indicates the average of the number of issues of each state for the seven days before the date and then divides the result by seven.

- **Analysis**: This report helps find the following aspects for issues that occur during the iteration in the team:
  - The frequency at which the team identifies issues
  - The team's progress with regard to fixing issues

If the team identifies more issues than it can address, the **Issue Trends** report will show the team as closing issues more slowly. The team might need to re-examine priorities to determine whether the issues are actually problems that it should address or whether they can be ignored.

- **Update and customization**: To update and customize the **Issue trends** report, open the Excel report file named **Issue Trends** in edit mode from the SharePoint document library named **Excel Reports**. By changing the following filter options of the PivotTable, the report gets customized in line with your requirement:

    ° To view the **Issue Trends** graph for the iteration, edit the **Work Item Iteration Hierarchy** filter option, which is selected by default as **All**

    ° To view the **Issue Trends** graph for a product area, edit the **Work Item Area Hierarchy** filter option, which is selected by default as **All**

    ° To view the **Issue Trends** graph for a specific interval, edit the **Rows/Columns** field from the PivotTable field list by specifying the particular interval

 For more information about the Project Management Dashboard and tracking work items, go to: `http://msdn.microsoft.com/en-us/library/dd420557.aspx`

Bug Backlog Management Excel reports

Bug Backlog Management reports are used to trace the bugs that the team has identified and the progress that the team has made in fixing them. These reports are available in the **Bugs** dashboard on the SharePoint site, that is associated with the team project portal.

Team members use the **Bugs** dashboard to determine if they are controlling the list of active bugs according to the defined team goals and agile process methodology. By unit-testing each addition of code before check-in, the team can diminish the number of bugs.

In order to have accurate data in the Bugs dashboard's Excel reports, team members need to perform the following activities in TFS:

- Defining bugs
- Specifying the iteration and area paths
- Specifying the priority of each bug
- Updating the status of each bug

 For more information about the Bugs Dashboard, go to `http://msdn.microsoft.com/en-us/library/dd560860.aspx`.

In the following sections, we will learn about the reports that are useful for monitoring the bug activity of the project and are available on the Bugs dashboard.

The Bug Progress report

The **Bug Progress** report is used to determine the team's progress towards fixing bugs. This Bug progress report is used to figure out how successful the team has been at discovering, resolving, and finishing the bugs. The following are the characteristics of the Bug Progress report

- **Chart description**: The **Bug Progress** report is a graphical view of the aggregated count of all the bugs, paired by their state for the last four weeks. This report represents the number of bugs in each state throughout the iteration of the last four weeks, as indicated in the following screenshot:

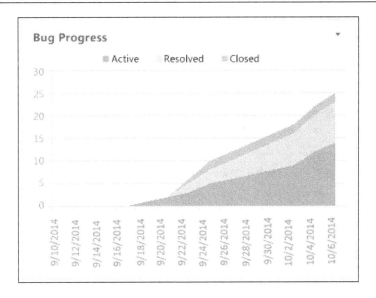

In the preceding graph, the x axis indicates days from the past four weeks, and the y axis indicates the bug item count.

- **Analysis**: This report helps determine the following aspects of bug progress throughout the iteration in the team:
    - The speed of resolving and fixing the bugs
    - Whether the speed of resolving bugs by the team is satisfactory
    - The bugs found by the team in the past days, if any

- **Update and customization**: To update and customize the **Bug Progress** report, open the Excel report file named **Bug Progress** in edit mode from the SharePoint document library named **Excel Reports**. By changing the following filter options of the PivotTable, the report gets customized in line with your requirements:
    - To view the **Bug Progress** graph for the iteration, edit the **Work Item Iteration Hierarchy** filter option, which is selected by default as **All**
    - To view the **Bug Progress** graph for a product area, edit the **Work Item Area Hierarchy** filter option, which is selected by default as **All**
    - To view the **Bug Progress** graph for a specific interval, edit the **Rows/ Columns** field from **PivotTable Field List** by specifying a particular set of weeks

The Bug Trends report

The **Bug Trends** report is used to trace the rate at which the team is finding, fixing, and resolving bugs. The following are the characteristics of the **Bug Trends** report:

- **Chart description**: The Bug Trends report is a line chart that represents the running average of the number of bugs that the team has opened, resolved, and closed, as indicated in the following screenshot:

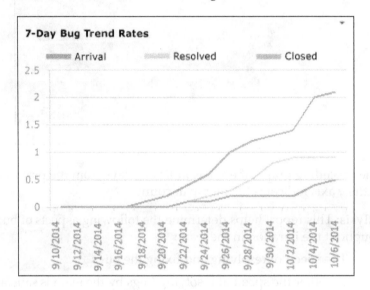

In the preceding graph, the x axis indicates days from the past four weeks, and the y axis indicates the running average based on the seven days prior to the date for which it is computed. In other words, the graph indicates the average of the number of bugs for each state for seven days before the date and then the divides the result by seven.

- **Analysis**: This report helps figure out the following aspects of bugs during the iteration in the team:
    - The frequency at which the team identifies bugs
    - The team's progress in fixing bugs

- **Update and customization**: To update and customize the Bug Trends report, open the Excel report file named **Bug Trends** in edit mode from the SharePoint document library named **Excel Reports**. By changing the following filter options of the PivotTable, the report gets customized in line with your requirements:

  ○ To view the bug trends graph for the iteration, edit the **Work Item Iteration Hierarchy** filter option, which is selected by default as **All**

  ○ To view the bug trends graph for a product area, edit the **Work Item Area Hierarchy** filter option, which is selected by default as **All**

  ○ To view the Bug Trends graph for a specific interval, edit the **Rows/Columns** field from the PivotTable Field List by specifying a set of weeks

The Bugs by Priority Report

The **Bugs by Priority** report is used to determine the number of active bugs and classify them by priority. It also helps figure out how successful the team has been at discovering, resolving, and finishing the bugs.

- **Chart description**: The **Bugs by Priority** report is a visual representation of the cumulative count of all bugs, grouped by their priority for the past four weeks. This report shows the distribution of active bugs, which are grouped by priority, as indicated in the following screenshot:

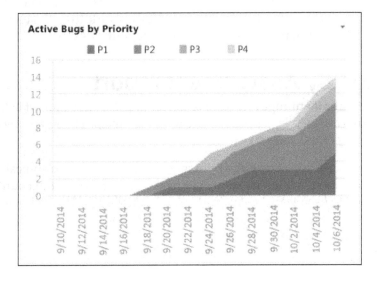

In the preceding graph, the x axis indicates days from the past four weeks, and the y axis indicates the bug item count.

- **Analysis**: This report helps to determine the following aspects of bug progress work throughout the sprint iteration in project team:
  - The number of active prioritized bugs
  - Whether bugs resolutions are in line with the priority sequence

- **Update and customization**: To update and customize the **Bugs by Priority** report, open the Excel report file named **Bugs by Priority** in edit mode from the SharePoint document library named **Excel Reports**. By changing the following filter options of the PivotTable, the report gets customized inline with your requirements:
  - To view the bugs by priority graph for the iteration, edit the **Work Item Iteration Hierarchy** filter option, which is selected by default as **All**
  - To view the bugs by priority graph for a product area, edit the **Work Item Area Hierarchy** filter option, which is selected by default as **All**
  - To view the bugs according to severity, replace the **Priority** column in the PivotTable field list with the severity
  - To view bugs by priority for a specific interval, edit the **Rows/Columns** field from the PivotTable field list by specifying a set of weeks
  - To view the graph for bugs by priority for specific states, such as active/resolved/closed bugs, edit the **Work Item System_State** filter option, which is selected by default as **Active**

The Bugs by Assignment report

The **Bugs by Assignment** report is used to determine the allocation of active bugs, which are classified by priority to the team members. The following are the characteristics of the **Bugs by Assignment** report:

- **Chart description**: The **Bugs by Assignment** report is a graphical representation, made via horizontal bar charts, of the overall count of bugs assigned to each team member in an active state, which are classified by priority, as indicated in the following screenshot:

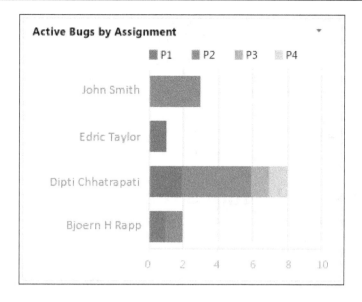

In the preceding graph, the x axis indicates the bug item count, and the y axis indicates the team member names.

- **Analysis**: This report helps determine the following aspects of bug progress throughout the sprint iteration in the project team:
  - ° The number of bugs allocated to each team member
  - ° Identification of the team member who has the most high-priority bugs
  - ° Identification of the team member who has a backlog of high-priority bugs

- **Update and customization**: To update and customize the **Bugs by Assignment** report, open the Excel report file named **Bugs by Assignment** in edit mode from the SharePoint document library named **Excel Reports**. By changing the following filter options of the PivotTable, the report gets customized as in line with your requirements:
  - ° To view the graph for allocated bugs as per the iteration, edit the **Work Item Iteration Hierarchy** filter option, which is selected by default as **All**
  - ° To view the graph for a product area's allocated bugs, edit the **Work Item Area Hierarchy** filter option, which is selected by default as **All**

- ° To view the graph for allocated bugs according to the severity, replace the **Priority** column in the PivotTable field list with the severity

- ° To view the graph for bugs by priority of a specific interval, edit the **Rows/Columns** field from the PivotTable field list by specifying a particular set of weeks

- ° To view the graph for allocated bugs of specific states, such as active/ resolved/closed bugs, edit the **Work Item System_State** filter option, which is selected by default as **Active**

The Bug Reactivations report

The **Bugs Reactivations** report is used to figure out how productively the team is resolving bugs. The following are the characteristics of the Bug Reactivations report:

The **Bug Reactivations** report appears on the **Quality** dashboard as well as on the SharePoint site. This dashboard combines the following Excel reports:

- The Test Plan Progress report
- The Build Status report
- The Bug Progress report
- The Bug Reactivations report
- The Code Coverage report
- The Code Churn report

- **Chart description**: The **Bug Reactivations** report is represented as a stacked area graph for the number of bugs that have been reactivated from among the fixed or closed bugs within the last four weeks, as indicated in the following screenshot:

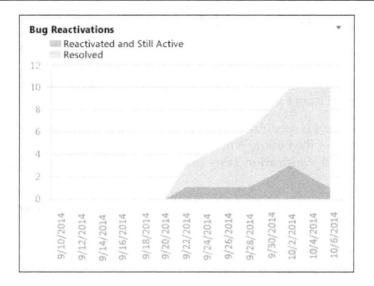

In the preceding graph, the x axis indicates days from the past four weeks, and the y axis indicates the bug item count.

- **Analysis**: This report helps determine the following aspects of bugs during the iteration in the team:
    - The number of reactivated bugs
    - The speed in resolving reactivated bugs

- **Update and customization**: To update and customize the **Bugs Reactivations** report, open the Excel report file named **Bug Reactivations** in edit mode from the SharePoint document library named **Excel Reports**. By changing the following filter options the PivotTable, the report gets customized in line with your requirements:
    - To view graph of reactivated bugs for the iteration, edit the **Work Item Iteration Hierarchy** filter option, which is selected by default as **All**
    - To view the graph for reactivated bugs of a product area, edit the **Work Item Area Hierarchy** filter option, which is selected by default as **All**
    - To view the graph for reactivated bugs for a specific interval, edit the **Rows/Columns** field from the PivotTable field list by specifying a set of weeks

Build Management Excel reports

Build Management Excel reports are used to track how source files get changed throughout the iteration and how strong the source code is while its being tested. These reports are represented on the **Build** dashboard on the SharePoint site that is associated with the team's project portal.

The **Build** dashboard is specifically used to analyze development activities that impact the quality of the builds. When builds are not successfully completed or aren't passing **Build Verification Tests (BVT)**, the team must resolve the problem instantly.

In order to have accurate reports for build management, team members need to complete the following activities:

- Configuring the build system
- Creating the build definitions
- Defining the tests to run automatically as part of the build
- Configuring the tests to gather code coverage data
- Running the builds regularly

For more information about build definition management, refer to the following links:

- http://msdn.microsoft.com/en-us/library/ms252495.aspx
- http://msdn.microsoft.com/en-us/library/ms181715.aspx
- http://msdn.microsoft.com/en-us/library/ms181716.aspx
- http://msdn.microsoft.com/en-us/library/ms181721.aspx

Also, team members can manually rate a build through the build explorer. The build rating shows up in the **Build Summary** report. This report is not part of the Build dashboard, but it can be added and customized as required.

For more information about the **Build Summary** report and **Quality** dashboard, refer to the following links:

- `http://msdn.microsoft.com/en-us/library/dd380708.aspx`

- `http://msdn.microsoft.com/en-us/library/dd420562.aspx`

- `http://msdn.microsoft.com/en-us/library/dd380683.aspx`

The project team can use the **Build** dashboard to observe the build's quality and the level of code coverage that they examine. Generally, the code coverage is higher and the code churn is lower. In accordance with the team's goals, the code coverage range should be 80-100 percent.

In the following sections, we will cover reports that monitor the build activity of the project and reside in the **Build** dashboard.

The Code Coverage report

The **Code Coverage** report is used to analyze the amount of code that the team tests over time. The following are the characteristics of the **Code Coverage** report:

- **Chart description**: The **Code Coverage** report is a graphical representation made via a line chart that shows the percentage of tested code under **Build Verification Test** during the last four weeks, as indicated in the following screenshot:

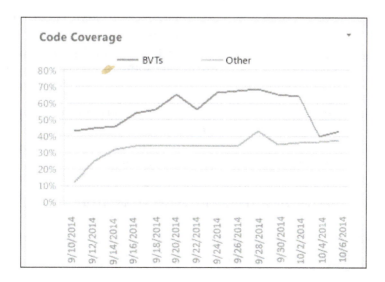

In the preceding graph, the x axis indicates days from the past four weeks, and the y axis indicates the precentage of BVT code coverage.

- **Analysis**: This report helps determine the following aspects of build work throughout the iteration in the project team:
  - Quantifying code tested by the team
  - Identifying sufficient code coverage by the team
  - Identifying increases/decreases in code coverage over time

- **Update and customization**: To update and customize the **Code Coverage** report, open the Excel report file named **Code Coverage** in edit mode from the SharePoint document library named **Excel Reports**. By changing the following filter options in the PivotTable, the report gets customized in line with your requirements:
  - To view the graph for code coverage of the iteration, edit the **Work Item. Iteration Hierarchy** filter option, which is selected by default as **All**
  - To view the graph for code coverage of a product area, edit the **Work Item Area Hierarchy** filter option, which is selected by default as **All**
  - To view the graph for code coverage of a specific interval, edit the **Rows/Columns** field from the PivotTable field list by specifying a set of weeks

The Code Churn report

The **Code Churn** report is used to determine and analyze source code files that change throughout the iterations. The Code churn report is best used to evaluate the amount of change that is taking place in the project. Ideally, high levels of code churn illustrate a weak project. The following are the characteristics of the **Code Churn** report:

- **Chart description**: The **Code Churn** report is a graphical representation depicted as a stacked area chart, and that shows the number of code lines that the team has added, deleted, and updated during check-ins before the build in the past four weeks, as indicated in the following screenshot:

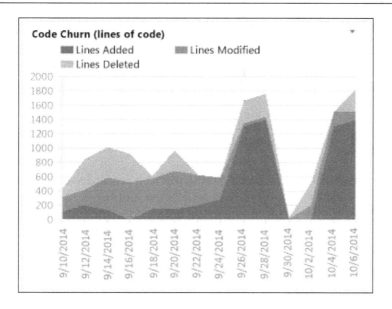

In the preceding graph, the x axis indicates days from the past four weeks, and the y axis indicates the line count.

- **Analysis**: This report helps determine the following aspects of build work throughout the iteration in the project team:
    - ° Quantifying the code tested by the team
    - ° Identifying sufficient tested code by the team
    - ° Predicting whether the targeted goals will be met

- **Update and customization**: To update and customize the **Code Churn** report, open the Excel report file named **Code Churn** in the mode from the SharePoint document library named **Excel Report**. By changing the following filter options of the PivotTable, the report gets customized in line with your requirements:

    - ° To view the graph for the code churn of the iteration, edit the **Work Item Iteration Hierarchy** filter option, which is selected by default as **All**

    - ° To view the graph for the code churn of a product area, edit the **Work Item Area Hierarchy** filter option, which is selected by default as **All**

    - ° To view the graph for the code churn of a specific interval, edit the **Rows/Columns** field from the PivotTable field list by specifying a set of weeks

The Build Status report

The **Build Status** report is used to track the progress of team builds by displaying the number of failed or successful builds in the last four weeks. The following are the characteristics of the **Build Status** report:

 The **Build Status** report appears on the **Quality** dashboard.

- **Chart description**: The **Build Status** report is a graphical representation made via a stacked column that depicts the number of failed or successful builds within the last four weeks, as indicated in the following screenshot:

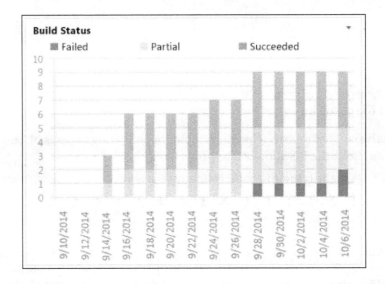

In the preceding graph, the *x* axis indicates days from the past four weeks, and the *y* axis indicates the build detail count.

- **Analysis**: This report helps determine the following aspects of build work during the iteration in the team:
  - Health of the team's builds
  - Identifying builds that need to be focused on

- **Update and customization**: To update and customize the **Build Status** report, open the Excel report file named **Build Status** in edit mode from the SharePoint document library named **Excel Reports**. By changing the following filter options in the PivotTable, the report gets customized in line with your requirements:

    ° To view the graph for build results for the iteration, edit the **Work Item Iteration Hierarchy** filter option, which is selected by default as **All**

    ° To view the graph for build results of a product area, edit the **Work Item Area Hierarchy** filter option, which is selected by default as **All**

    ° To view the graph for build results of a specific interval, edit the **Rows/Columns** field from the PivotTable Field List by specifying a set of weeks

Test Management Excel reports

Test Management Excel reports are used to analyze test activities, provide information on progress, find out the areas lacking in test scope, and determine areas that might require review. These reports are represented on the **Test Dashboard** on the SharePoint site that is associated with the team's project portal. This dashboard offers five reports that provide details about test activities that happened in the last four weeks.

In order to have accurate data about the Test dashboard's Excel reports, team members need to perform the following activities in TFS:

- Planning and creating user stories

- Planning and creating test cases

- Generating **Tested By** links from test cases to user stories

- Deciding test plans and assigning test cases to test plans

- For manual tests, marking each validation step's result in passed or failed test cases

- To filter the data, updating each test case with iteration and area paths

 Testers must mark a test step with a status if it is a validation test step. The overall result for a test case reflects the status of all the test steps that the tester marks. Therefore, the test case has a status of failed if the tester has marked any test step as failed or not marked it. Also, in automated tests, each test case is automatically marked as passed or failed.

In order to show data on the test dashboard, the test team needs to test the application through a test runner and Microsoft Test Manager. Moreover, these reports need the team's project to be established via reporting services. To view this report, the designated team member must be assigned the **Browser** role permission in reporting services. Data for Test Management Excel reports fetched from the data warehouse and the test results are generated by Microsoft Test Manager.

> For more information about organizing test cases for the test dashboard and Reporting Service reports, refer to the following links:
>
> - http://msdn.microsoft.com/en-us/library/dd380763.aspx
> - http://msdn.microsoft.com/en-us/library/dd380714.aspx
> - http://msdn.microsoft.com/en-us/library/dd286725.aspx
> - http://msdn.microsoft.com/en-us/library/dd420548.aspx

In the following section, we will learn about reports that are useful for monitoring the test activity of the project; these are available on the **Test** dashboard.

The Test Plan Progress report

The **Test plan Progress** report is used to trace the team's progress in testing the application. The following are the characteristics of the **Test Plan Progress** report:

- **Chart description**: The Test Plan Progress report is a graphical representation made with a stacked area graph of the test results (such as **Never Run**, **Blocked**, **Failed**, or **Passed**) in the last four weeks, as indicated in the following screenshot:

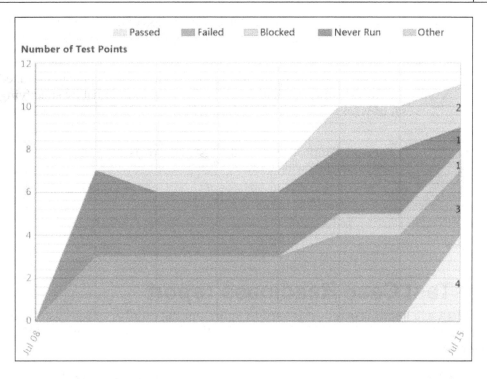

In the preceding graph, the x axis indicates the days in a sprint or iteration, and the y axis indicates test points.

- **Analysis**: This report helps determine the following aspects of test cases for the team project:
    - ° Quantifying the team's testing process
    - ° The progress made by the team in testing
    - ° Identifying the number of remaining tests
    - ° Identifying passed, failed, and blocked tests

- **Update and customization**: To update and customize the Test Plan Progress report, open the Excel report file named **Test Plan Progress** in edit mode from the SharePoint document library named **Excel Reports**. By changing the following filter options of the PivotTable, the report gets customized in line with your requirements:
    - ° To view the graph for the test plan progress of the iteration, edit the **Work Item Iteration Hierarchy** filter option, which is selected by default as **All**

- ○ To view the graph for the test plan progress of a product area, edit the **Work Item Area Hierarchy** filter option, which is selected by default as **All**

- ○ To view the graph for the test plan progress of a specific interval, edit the **Rows/Columns** field from the PivotTable field list by specifying a set of weeks

For more information about the Test plan progress report, refer to the following links:

- `http://msdn.microsoft.com/en-us/library/dd286682.aspx`

- `http://msdn.microsoft.com/en-us/library/dd380702.aspx`

The Test Case Readiness report

The **Test Case Readiness** report is used to figure out the number of test cases that are defined and ready to run. The following are the characteristics of the **Test Case Readiness** report:

- **Chart description**: The **Test Case Readiness** report is a graphical representation made with a stacked area graph that represents the number of designed and ready test cases in the last four weeks, as indicated in the following screenshot:

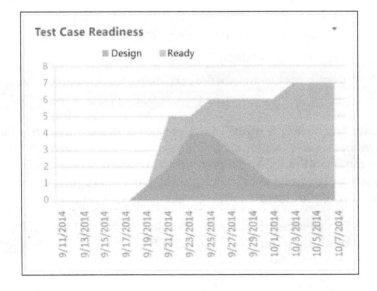

The preceding graph summarizes the data that was captured for each test case during the time interval. Also, the *x* axis indicates days from the last four weeks and the *y* axis indicates the test case work item count.

- **Analysis**: This report helps determine the following aspects of test cases for the team's project:

    ○ A prediction about tests that will be run in the future

    ○ A prediction about the readiness of the test cases

    ○ The number of remaining test cases

    ○ The number of ready test cases

- **Update and customization**: To update and customize the **Test Case Readiness** report, open the Excel report file named **Test Case Readiness** in edit mode from the SharePoint document library named **Excel Reports**. By changing the following filter options of the PivotTable, the report gets customized in line with your requirements:

    ○ To view the graph for test case readiness of the iteration, edit the **Work Item Iteration Hierarchy** filter option, which is selected by default as **All**

    ○ To view the graph for the test case readiness of a product area, edit the **Work Item Area Hierarchy** filter option, which is selected by default as **All**

 For more information about the **Test Case Readiness** report, go to http://msdn.microsoft.com/en-us/library/dd380713.aspx.

The User Story Test Status report

The **User Story Test Status** report is used to find out any lack in the test scope and determine the test progress of the user story. The following are the characteristics of the **User Story Status** report:

- **Chart description**: The **User Story Test Status** report is a graphical representation made with a horizontal bar chart that represents the number of test results for the test case and the test configuration aggregation that is created for each user story. The chart classifies the test results in line with the most recent test run (for example, **Passed** is shown in green, **Failed** in red, **Blocked** in purple, or **Never Run** in gray), as indicated in the following screenshot:

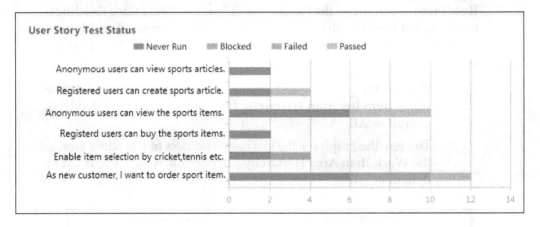

In the preceding graph, the x axis indicates the test case item count, and the y axis indicates the user story.

- **Analysis**: This report helps determine the following aspects of test cases for the team project:
  - Identifying user stories with a low count of test cases
  - Identifying user stories with a high total count of Blocked or Never run test cases
  - The test case scope for the user story
  - The user story with a high rate of test failures
  - The average number of test cases defined per user story
  - The team's work progress with respect to test cases for each user story
  - Understanding test case block issues and addressing them

- **Update and customization**: To update and customize the **User Story Test Status** report, open the Excel report file named **User Story Test Status** in edit mode from the SharePoint document library named **Excel Reports**. By changing the following filter options of the PivotTable, the report gets customized in line with your requirements:

  ° To view the graph for user story test status of the iteration, edit the **Work Item Iteration Hierarchy** filter option, which is selected by default as **All**

  ° To view the graph for the user story test status of a product area, edit the **Work Item Area Hierarchy filter** option, which is selected by default as **All**

The Test Activity report

The **Test Activity** report is used to determine the number of manual tests that the team has run throughout the iterations. The following are the characteristics of the **Test Activity** report:

- **Chart description**: The **Test Activity** report is a graphical representation made via a line chart that depicts the aggregate count of all manual test results in the last four weeks, as indicated in the following screenshot:

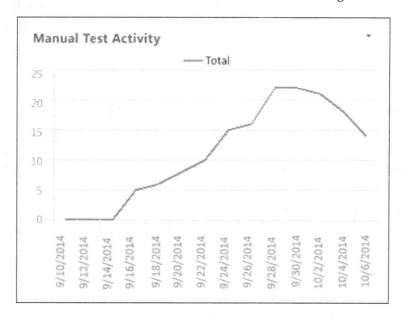

In the preceding graph, the x axis indicates days from the last four weeks and the y axis indicates the test case result count.

- **Analysis**: This report helps determine the following aspects of test activities for the team project:
    - ° Manual test variations
    - ° Identifying spikes
    - ° The status of recent builds, bug status, and code churn

- **Update and customization**: To update and customize the **Test Plan Progress** report, open the Excel report file named **Test Activity** in the edit mode from the SharePoint document library named **Excel Reports**. By changing the following filter options of the PivotTable, the report gets customized in line with your requirements:
    - ° To view the graph for the test activity of the iteration, edit the **Work Item Iteration Hierarchy** filter option, which is selected by default as **All**
    - ° To view the graph for a product area's test activity, edit the **Work Item Area Hierarchy** filter option, which is selected by default as **All**
    - ° To view the graph of test activity for a specific test plan, edit the **Test Plan Name** filter option, which is selected by default as **All**
    - ° To view the graph for the test activity of automated test cases, edit the **Is Automated** filter option, which is selected by default as **False**
    - ° To view the graph for a specific interval's test activity, edit the **Rows/Columns** field from the PivotTable Field List by specifying a set of weeks

The Test Failure Analysis report

The **Failure Analysis** report is used to determine the number of regressions by the test team. This report represents the number of distinct configurations for each previously passed test case that is failing since the last four weeks. The following are the characteristics of the **Test Failure Analysis** report:

- **Chart description**: The **Test Failure Analysis** report is a graphical representation made via a stacked area graph that depicts the aggregated count of all failed outcome results for tests such as Regression, New Issue, or Known Issue in the last four weeks, as indicated in the following screenshot:

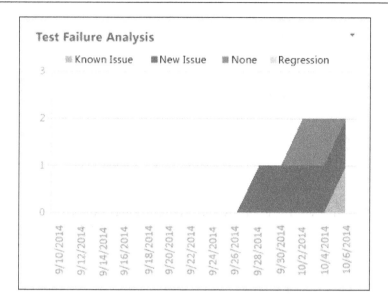

In the preceding graph, the *x* axis indicates days from the last four weeks, and the *y* axis indicates the test points.

- **Analysis**: This report helps determine the following aspects of regressions for the team project:
    - Overall tests that are regressing
    - The progress of the regression test
    - Verifying issue identification by the team
    - The status of the latest builds, bug status, and code churn
    - Identifying spikes if occurred

- **Update and customization**: To update and customize the **Test Failure Analysis** report, open the Excel report file named **Failure Analysis** in edit mode from the SharePoint document library named **Excel Reports**. By changing the following filter options of the PivotTable, the report gets customized in line with your requirements:
    - To view the graph for the failure analysis of the iteration, edit the **Work Item Iteration Hierarchy** filter option, which is selected by default as **All**

- ° To view the graph for the failure analysis of a product area, edit the **Work Item Area Hierarchy** filter option, which is selected by default as **All**

- ° To view the graph for the failure analysis for a specific test plan, edit the **Test Plan Name** filter option, which is selected by default as **All**

- ° To view the graph of failure analysis for a specific interval, edit the **Rows/Columns** field from the PivotTable field list by specifying a set of weeks

Summary

In this chapter, we got a basic understanding of integration between SharePoint 2013 and TFS 2013. We also learned about different types of Excel reports and how to customize them in line with different types of dashboards.

In the next chapter, we will learn to create SSRS reports.

4
SQL Server Reporting

This chapter briefly examines the tools available to create and customize reports using **Report Definition Language** (**RDL**). Team Foundation Server 2013 includes a set of out-of-the-box RDL reports. These reports vary by the type of process template you choose to use for your project. This chapter will demonstrate how to create RDL reports using two main tools for this purpose: **SQL Server Report Builder** and **Report Designer**. SQL reports in TFS 2013 allow for much more detailed reports than Excel reporting.

This chapter covers the following topics:

- SQL Server Reporting Services
- SQL Server Reporting Tools
- Understanding default SQL reports
- Creating custom SQL reports

SQL Server Reporting Services

It's better to understand the intercommunication between TFS, SQL Server, and SQL Server Reporting Services in order to create and customize reports in TFS using SQL Reporting Services. TFS databases reside in the SQL server to store configuration information, all information for the reports, and team project data information.

TFS uses SQL Server for the following purposes:

- To load work items, test results, and build results into SQL Server
- To aggregate and analyze report data
- To drive reports

SQL Server Reporting Services makes available created by the process template or by the respective team members. SQL **Reporting Service Reports** is a good choice for highly formatted, scalable, manageable, and consistent reports. To integrate the reporting service on TFS, SQL Reporting Service Reports requires the following configuration setup:

- Installing SQL Server 2014 Reporting Services and Analysis Services
- Configuring SQL Reporting Services
- Enabling Reporting and Analysis Service in TFS

After integrating SQL reporting service on TFS, a team member can benefit from default SQL reports to observe Burndown, build quality, bug trends, and test progress, as indicated in following screenshot:

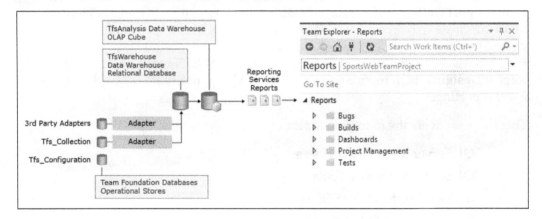

The next topic explains the reporting tools that are used to update an existing report or to create a new one.

SQL Server reporting tools

SQL Reporting Services offers two important tools, namely Report Builder and Report Designer, that help to create and deploy reports. These tools are basically used to create RDL files to represent the report on Report Manager. Both reporting tools point to the `Tfs_Analysis` and `TFS_Warehouse` databases. They help in creating consistent and sophisticated reports by adding bar charts, indicators, or spark lines as required.

The following figure illustrates the connection between reporting tools in Reporting Service:

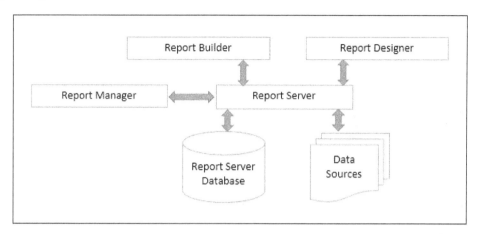

Report Server is the central component of the Reporting Service's installation. It consists of a pair of report processors that execute the reports present in the server. Also, it consists of a collection of special-purpose extensions that handle authentication, data processing, rendering, and delivery operations. So, basically, it's a core engine that drives Reporting Services. Report Manager provides web-based report access and management capabilities. The default URL that invokes Report Manager is http://<<Report Server>>/reports. Report Builder provides drag-and-drop and an easy-to-use report design functionality. Report Designer allows developers to develop complex reports. It's an extensive report authoring and publishing tool that can be executed on a client machine. Report Server Databases store reporting data such as report definitions, report history, report metadata, cached reports, resources, snapshots, scheduling and delivery data, encrypted data, and security settings.

Report Builder

The Report Builder tool fully supports SQL Reporting Services and provides a Microsoft-Office-like report-authoring environment. SQL Server 2012 SP1 and SQL Server 2014 include Report Builder 3.0. Report Builder is designed for business analysts and developers who want to create custom reports quickly and easily.

With this tool, you can work with RDL files, make the necessary changes, and save them as an RDL file. After installing the tool, launch Report Builder and start by connecting to the Report Server (for example, http://<yourservername>/reportserver).

Report Builder is capable of visualizing data that includes reporting information that helps to create vision beyond the chart and tables.

For more information on Report Builder, go to:
https://technet.microsoft.com/en-us/library/dd220460

Report Designer

Report Designer is an integrated environment for the development of cubes (a cube is a set of data that is usually constructed from a subset of a data warehouse and is organized and summarized into a multidimensional structure), data sources, and reports. It is a much more complex tool than Report Builder, but it gives you the ability to create highly complex and rich reports.

Report Designer 3.0 is hosted over Business Intelligence Development, which is a user-friendly interface for the creation of robust reports that include data from multiple types of data sources. In Visual Studio, reports are saved as client report definition (.rdlc) files. These files are based on the same schema as report definition (.rdl) files published on the SQL Server Reporting Services report servers, but they are stored and processed differently from .rdl files. At runtime, the .rdlc files are processed locally, while the .rdl files are processed remotely. In later sections, we will look further into creating custom reports using Report Builder and Business Intelligence Development Studio.

For more information on both reporting tools, refer to the following links:

- https://msdn.microsoft.com/library/dd207010.aspx
- https://technet.microsoft.com/en-us/library/ms159253(v=sql.105).aspx#RBRDFeatures

Understanding default SQL reports

Default reports are very useful for analyzing the progress and quality of a project throughout its application lifecycle. These reports display the information from work items, test results, version control, and builds. Default reports are basically RDL files that contain information about reporting layout and data source. RDS files do not contain actual reporting data, but they combine reporting data and layout during the reporting process and pass it to the report renderer.

If a team member has the required permission to view SQL reports, the Team Explorer in Visual Studio will appear with the default reports, as displayed in the following screenshot:

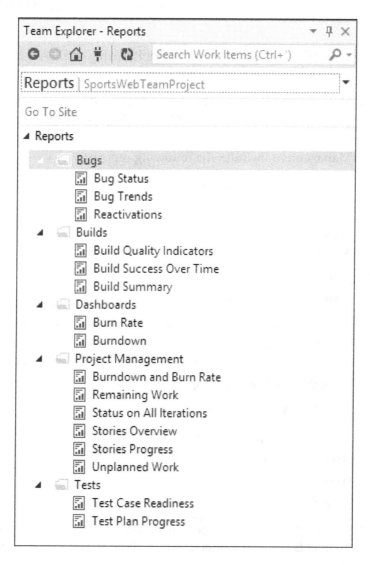

The reports page on Team Explorer shows the different reports under a set of folders in line with the process template. Here, we are referring to the Agile Process template and, hence, the report page shows only Agile SQL reports.

If SQL reports don't appear as expected, review the checklist as mentioned in the following URL:

`https://msdn.microsoft.com/en-us/library/jj920172.aspx`

The following default SQL repots are used to monitor code quality, work progress, test plans, and bug tracking in the team project:

- Project Management Reports: These reports provide a visualization of an ongoing work item's status and progress during the sprint cycle, which helps decide on for further activities.

  Project Management includes the following reports:

  - Burndown and Burn Rate report
  - Remaining Work report
  - Unplanned Work report
  - Status of All Iterations report
  - Stories Overview report
  - Stories Progress report

- Test and Bug Reports: Test reports are specifically used to learn about test progress and receive an analysis of user stories or backlog items, while bug reports are meant to analyze the team's capability to identify and fix the bugs

  Tests and bugs have the following reports:

  - Test Case Readiness report
  - Test Plan Progress report
  - Bug Status report
  - Bug Trends report
  - Reactivation report

- Build Reports: These reports record the quality of the software development. Build reports also give an understanding about the quality of code, tests, and builds

Build Reports contain the following reports:

- ° Build Quality Indicators
- ° Build Success Over Time
- ° Build Summary

 To understand each report in detail, go to:
https://msdn.microsoft.com/en-us/
library/bb649552.aspx

Default SQL reports are stored in Reporting Services, which you can access through Team Explorer or Report Manager. You can also include your own folder to specify custom reports under **Reports** in the **Team Explorer** window; this lets you organize reports more effectively.

To access reports via Team Explorer, choose any report from Team Explorer (say, the Bug Status report) and press the *Enter* key, as shown in the following screenshot:

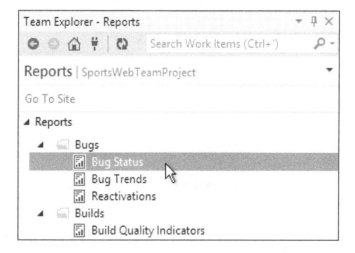

A web browser will open the report where you need to specify a parameter to include the desired content in the report. Click on **View Report**.

To access reports via **Report Manager**, choose **Reports** in the **Team Explorer** window and click on **Go To Site**, as indicated in the following screenshot:

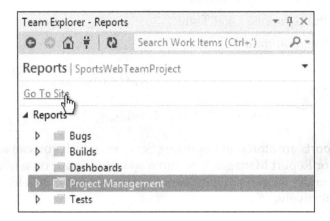

In **Report Manager**, select the folder that contains the report you want to monitor (say, the Builds report), as shown in following screenshot:

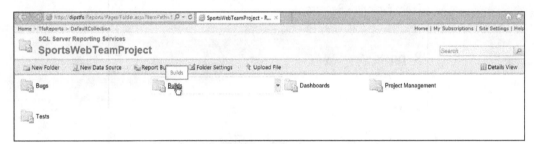

Next, choose the report you want to open, specify the filtering parameters, and click on **View Report**.

Creating custom SQL reports

We now have a little understanding about the purpose of SQL Server Reporting Tools. This section will walk you through the process of creating custom reports using Report Builder and Report Designer (Business Intelligence Development Studio).

Creating custom reports using Report Builder

Report Builder is a simple and easy report authoring tool for business users, which is supported by SQL Reporting services. Report Builder 3.0 provides the capability to design, execute, and deploy to SQL Server Reporting Services. The user interface has been streamlined to allow business users to become proficient at authoring reports very quickly.

To set up Report Builder 3.0, refer to the following links:

- `http://www.microsoft.com/en-in/download/details.aspx?id=42301`

- `https://technet.microsoft.com/en-us/library/dd207038(v=sql.120).aspx`

Once Report builder is successfully integrated, follow the ensuing steps to create a custom report to know the number of active work items per day for the specified month:

1. Open **Report Builder**, click the round button in the top-left corner, and click on **New** as shown:

2. Select **Table or Matrix Wizard** in the **New Report or Dataset** window as shown:

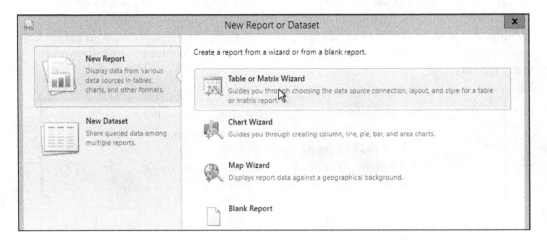

3. Choose **Create a dataset** and click on **Next**:

4. In the next window, click on the **New...** button and specify the name of the data source (say, **TfsOlapReportDS**):

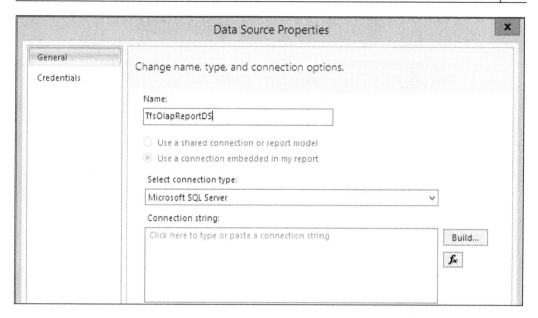

5. Now, click on the **Build...** button and then click on **Change** in the
    Connection Properties window:

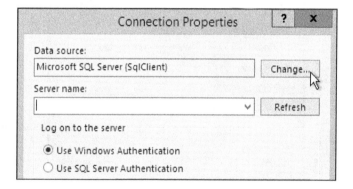

6. Select **Microsoft SQL Server Analysis Services** under **Data source** and click on **OK**.

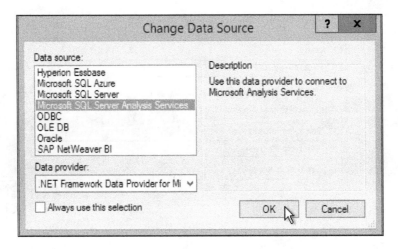

7. Next, specify the Reporting **Server name**, select the TFS Analysis database (**Tfs_TFSDBAnalysis**) and click on **OK**.

8. Verify the connection by clicking on **Test Connection** and then click on **OK**:

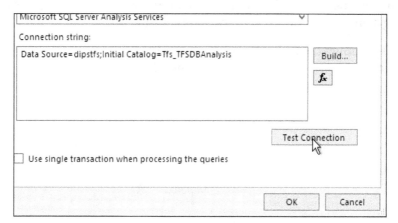

9. Now the data source connection has been established. Click on **Next**:

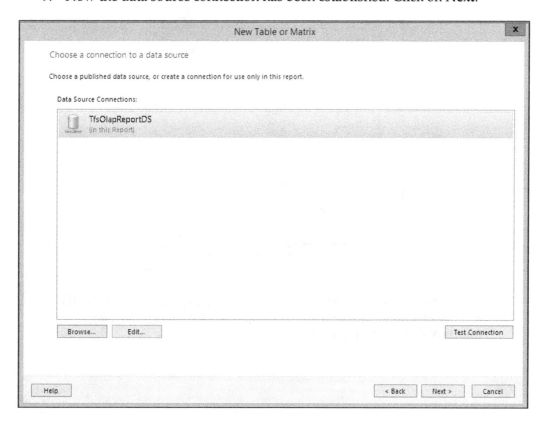

It's now time to design and build the query for the report. The prompted design query dialog box display the filters, rows, columns, and values to create the report. The ensuing steps allow you to build the query for the report:

1. Narrow down the query by selecting the Team project. Expand the **Team Project** group from the **Measures Group** list:

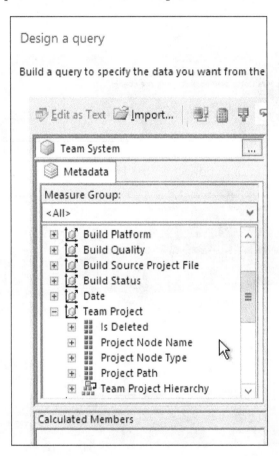

2. Drag-and-drop **Project Node Name** into the query builder and specify a parameter value in line with the desired team project name (say, **SportsWebTeamProject**):

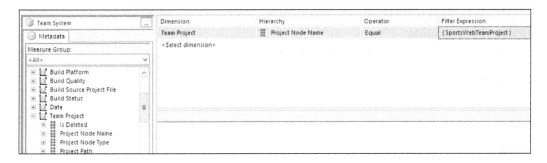

3. Expand the **Work Item** group under **Measure Group** and drag-and-drop **Work Item.System_WorkItemType** into the query builder:

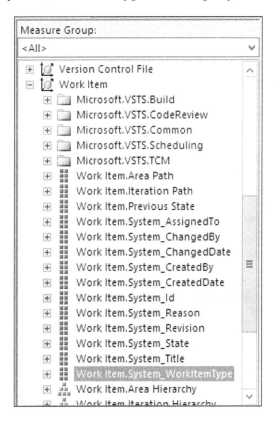

4. Specify the **Work Item.System_WorkItemType** filter as **Task** in the
   query builder.

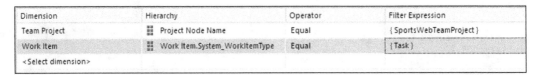

Dimension	Hierarchy	Operator	Filter Expression
Team Project	Project Node Name	Equal	{ SportsWebTeamProject }
Work Item	Work Item.System_WorkItemType	Equal	{ Task }
<Select dimension>			

5. To add a task count as the value by which to measure the report, expand
   the **Measure Groups** list and drag-and-drop **Work Item Count** in the folder
   levels under **Measures** here to add to the query box, which gives the total
   task value in the specified project:

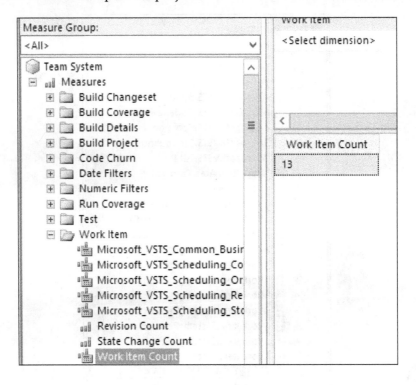

6. To show only the Active task, expand the **Work Item** group in the **Measure Group** list. Drag-and-drop **Work Item.System_State** into the query builder and set **Filter Expression** to **Active**. This will immediately update the value of the total tasks in the project:

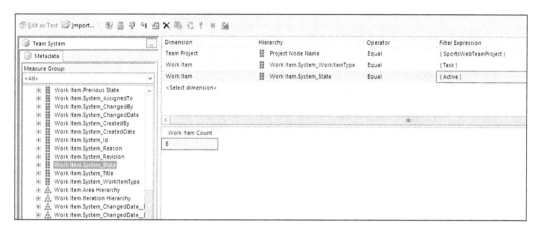

7. To specify the date range, expand the **Date** group in the **Measure Group** list. Drag-and-drop **Month** to the query builder and specify the **Month** and **Year** (for example, **October 2014**):

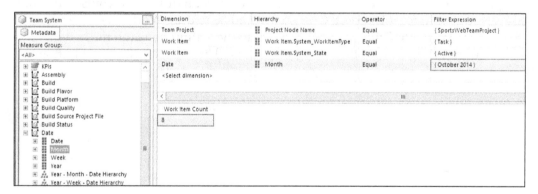

8. Now drag-and-drop the **Date** item under the **Date** group into the large box where the **Work Item Count** is displayed:

	Date	Work Item Count
⊞ Build Quality		
⊞ Build Source Project File	10/1/2014	3
⊞ Build Status	10/2/2014	3
⊟ Date	10/3/2014	3
⊞ Date		
⊞ Month	10/4/2014	3
⊞ Week		
⊞ Year	10/5/2014	3
⊞ Year - Month - Date Hierarchy	10/6/2014	12
⊞ Year - Week - Date Hierarchy		
⊞ Team Project	10/7/2014	8
⊞ Test Case	10/8/2014	8
⊞ Test Configuration		
⊞ Test Plan	10/9/2014	8
⊞ Test Result	10/10/2014	8
⊞ Test Run	10/11/2014	8

9. Now that the desired data has been specified, click on **Next** to format the report.

10. Now you can see that the **New Table or Matrix** dialog box is displayed. Depending on your preferences, there are several different layouts that could be chosen for this report. One way would be to drag **Work_Item_Count** in the **Available fields** pane (on the left) to the **Values** pane (on the bottom right). Drag **Date** to the **Row groups** pane. Then, click on the **Next** button.

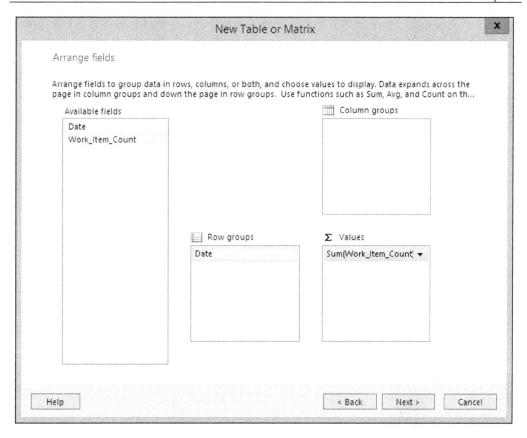

11. You can now see the **Choose the layout** dialog box. For this example, you can just directly click on **Next**.

12. Next the **Choose a style** dialog box appears, which is the final dialog box for the **New Table or Matrix wizard**. Click on **Finish**. The *design* of the report is now complete and is displayed as follows:

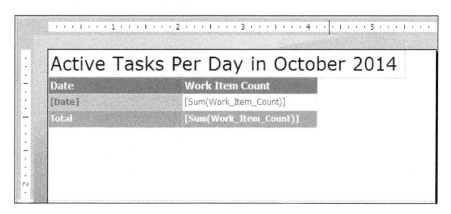

13. Click on the **Run** button in the upper-left-hand corner in the Report Builder. It will perform all the necessary calculations and database queries to gather the data and format it into the desired report, as follows:

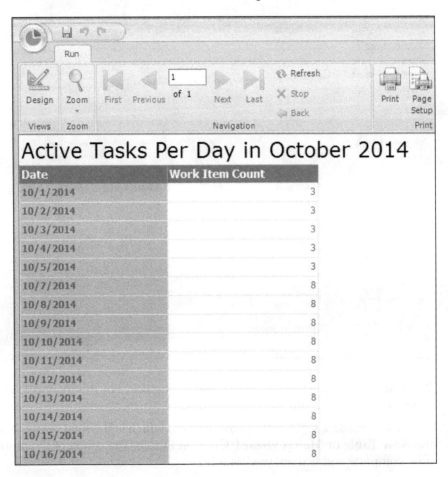

14. The last step is to save this report. Click on the icon in the upper-left-hand corner and select **Save** from the drop-down menu. Give the report a meaningful name (say, **Active Tasks_October 2014**) and click on **OK**:

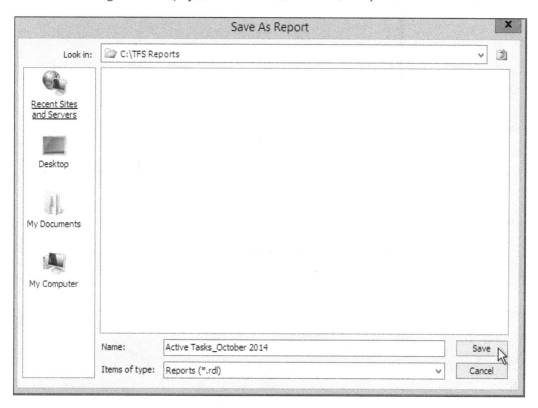

15. To display the report on the Reporting site, select **Reports** in **Team Explorer** and click on **Go To Site**:

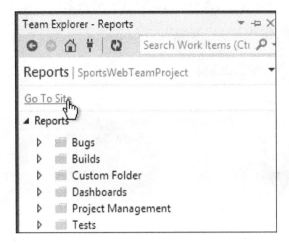

16. On the Reporting site, click on **Upload File**:

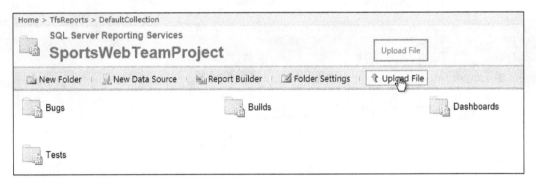

17. Click on **Browse** and go to the location where the report has been saved. Choose the report and click on **Open**:

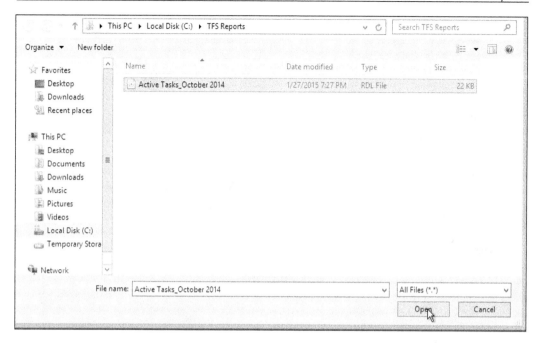

18. Click on **OK**, after which the report will be added in the list of already existing reports:

19. You should now see the customized report. It can be viewed by anyone who has the right to access the Team Reporting Site, as shown in the following screenshot:

Home > TfsReports > DefaultCollection > SportsWebTeamProject > Active Tasks_October 2014

| 1 | of 1 | 100% | Find | Next |

Active Tasks Per Day in October 2014

Date	Work Item Count
10/1/2014	3
10/2/2014	3
10/3/2014	3
10/4/2014	3
10/5/2014	3
10/7/2014	8
10/8/2014	8
10/9/2014	8
10/10/2014	8
10/11/2014	8
10/12/2014	8
10/13/2014	8
10/14/2014	8
10/15/2014	8
10/16/2014	8
10/17/2014	8
10/18/2014	8
10/19/2014	8
10/20/2014	8
10/21/2014	8

For more information about creating reports in Report Builder, go to:
https://msdn.microsoft.com/en-us/library/dd220460.aspx

Creating custom reports using Report Designer

As of now, we have constructed reports using Report Builder. However, another option is available; known as Report Designer, this is for the report creation feature integrated with Visual Studio. Report Designer requires the installation of Microsoft SQL Server Data Tools and needs to be configured with SQL Server.

To install and set up the environment for Report Designer, refer to the following links:

- http://www.microsoft.com/en-us/download/
  details.aspx?id=42313
- https://msdn.microsoft.com/en-us/library/
  jj856966(v=sql.120).aspx

Once the configuration has been done correctly, follow these steps to create custom reports:

1. Open Visual Studio and navigate to **File | New | Project...**:

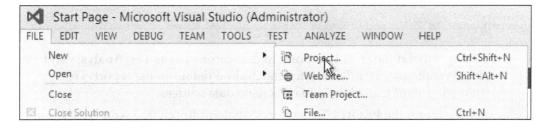

2. Select the **Report Server Project** template after navigating to **Business Intelligence | Reporting Service**. Click on **OK**:

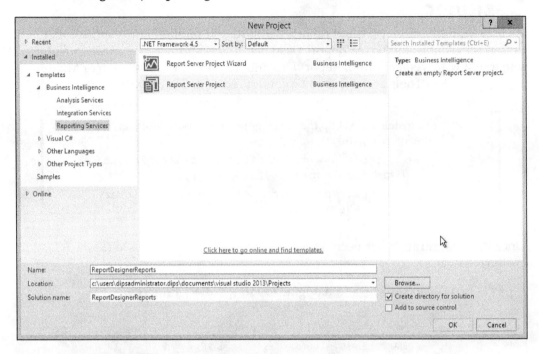

3. Create two data sources that point to databases such as **Tfs_Analysis** and **Tfs_Warehouse,** in order to fetch the desired details in the report. The following steps show how you can create data sources:

1. From the **PROJECT** menu in Visual Studio, choose **Add New Item**:

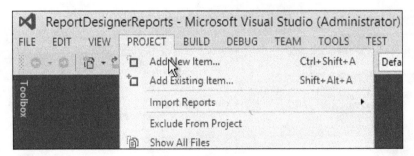

2. Select **Data source** and click on **Add**.

3. Specify the name of the data source (say, **TfsAnalysisReportDS**) and click on **Edit**:

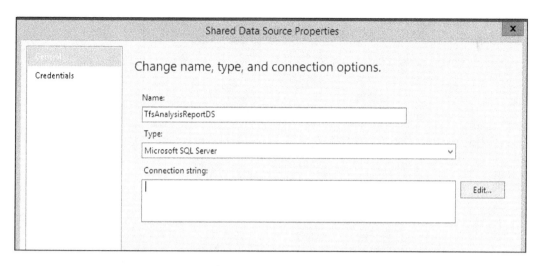

4. Click on **Change** in the **Connection Properties** window.

5. Select **Microsoft SQL Server Analysis Services** and click on **OK**.

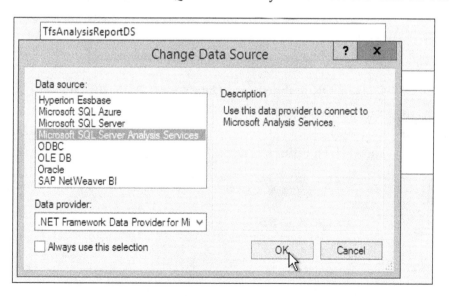

6. Specify the name of the Reporting Server, select a TFS Analysis database (say, **Tfs_TFSDBAnalysis**), and click on **OK**:

7. Click on **OK** in the **Shared Data Source Properties** window.

8. Repeat steps 1 and 2 to start creating the TFS warehouse data source.

9. Specify the name of the data source (say, **TfsWarehouseReportDS**) and click on **Edit**:

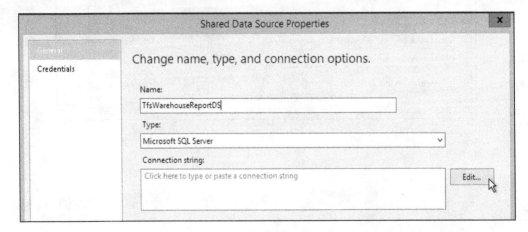

10. Specify the name of the Reporting Server, select a TFS Analysis database (say, **Tfs_TFSDBWarehouse**), and click on **OK**.

11. Click on **OK** in the **Shared Data Source Properties** window.

4. Specify the **TargetServerURL** address in the project properties as the Reporting Services server and click on **OK**:

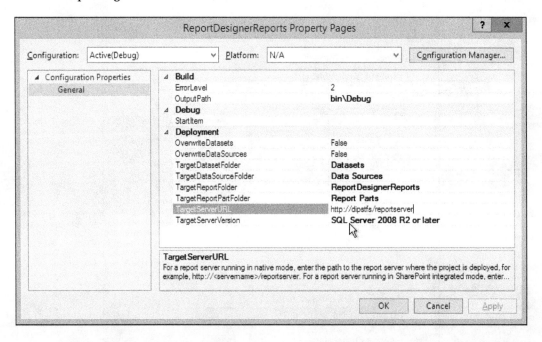

5. In the project, you will have the two data sources created earlier, as indicated in the following screenshot:

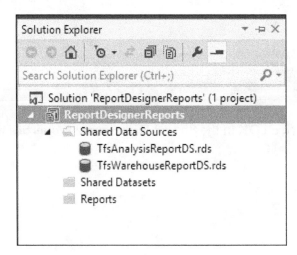

6. Now create a custom report using the TFS Warehouse database. Follow the steps given to create a custom report:

　　1. From the **PROJECT** menu in Visual Studio, choose **Add New Item**.

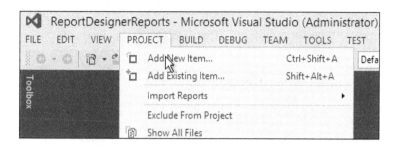

　　2. Select **Report Wizard** and click on **Add**:

3. In the next wizard, click on **Next**. Specify the TFS Warehouse Data source in the next window and click on **Next**:

4. Select **Query Builder** in the **Design the Query** page to build the custom query.

5. **Add the following tables in Query Designer:**
   - DimPerson
   - DimWorkItem
   - FactCurrentWorkItem

The following screenshot shows the Query Designer window:

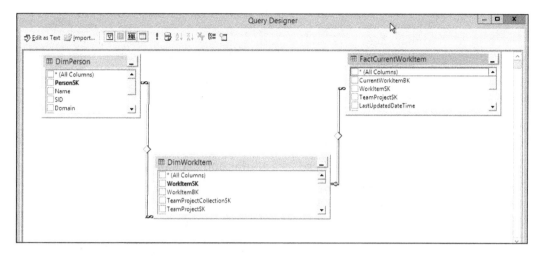

6. Design the query, as shown in following screenshot, to view all work items per state, and click on **OK**.

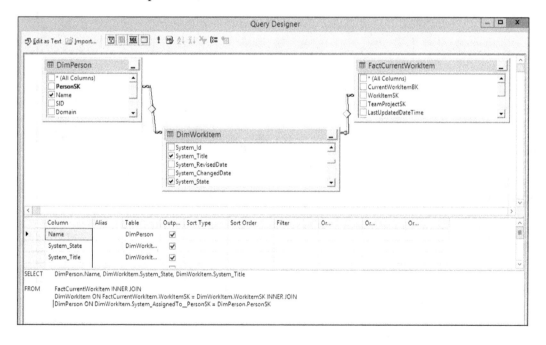

The fully updated query will be as follows:

```
SELECT   DimPerson.Name,
DimWorkItem.System_State,
DimWorkItem.System_Title
FROM          FactCurrentWorkItem INNER JOIN
DimWorkItem ON FactCurrentWorkItem.WorkItemSK =
DimWorkItem.WorkItemSK INNER JOIN
DimPerson ON DimWorkItem.System_AssignedTo__PersonSK =
DimPerson.PersonSK
```

7. Verify the query and click on **Next**.

8. Select the **Report Type** as **Tabular** and click on **Next**.

9. To design the report layout, drag-and-drop **Name** and **System_Title** into **Details**. Drag-and-drop **System_State** into **Group** and click on **Next**, as shown in the following screenshot:

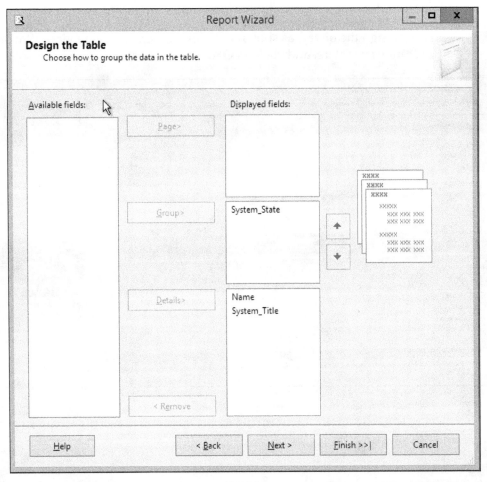

10. Keep the selection as it is and click on **Next**. Then, choose a style (for example, **Ocean**) for the table. Click on **Next**.

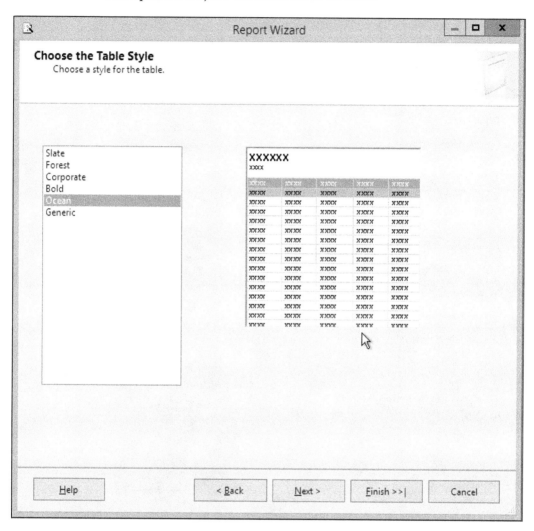

11. Name the report in the **Report name** fields and verify the **Report summary**. Then, click on **Finish** to complete the wizard:

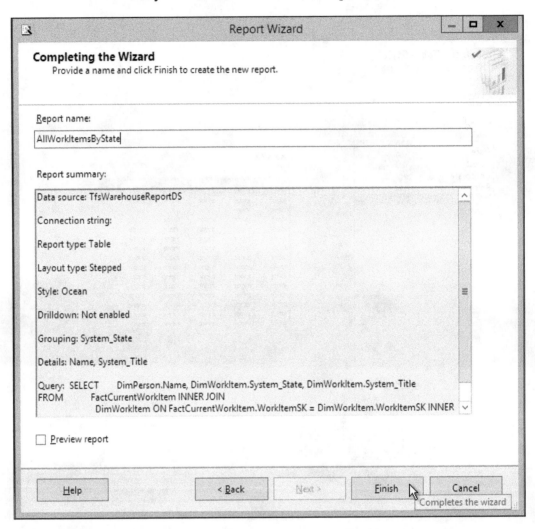

12. To deploy the report in Reporting Server, choose **Deploy Solution** from the **BUILD** menu:

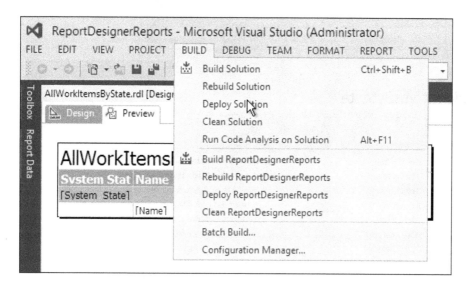

13. To view the report , open the Report Manager site where the report project has been deployed:

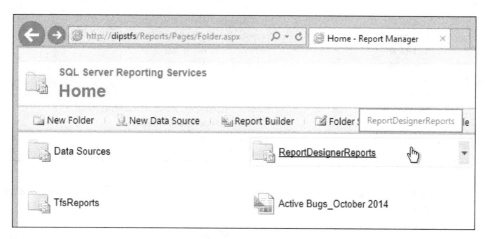

14. Click on the **Report Project** folder. Then, click on **Report** to view all the work items according to their state (**Active/Closed/New**):

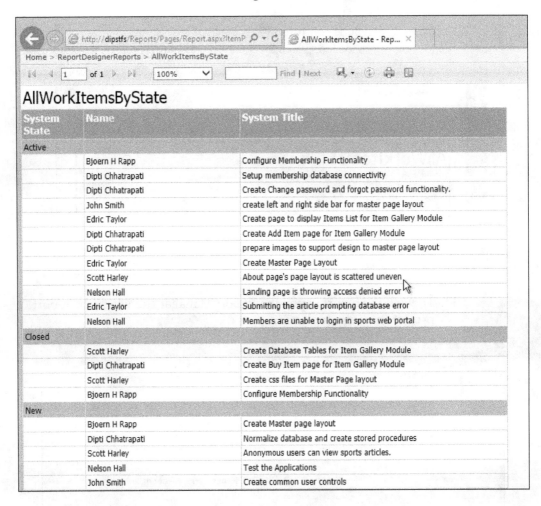

7. Next, to create an aggregated custom report using the TFS Analysis database, refer to the following steps:

1. From the **PROJECT** menu in Visual Studio, choose **Add New Item**.

2. Select **Report Wizard** and click on **Add**:

3. In the wizard, click on **Next**. Specify the TFS Analysis **Data Source** in the next window and click on **Next**:

4. Select **Query Builder** on the **Design the Query** page to build the custom query.

5. To customize the query further, and to create a query that will retrieve the data for the report, go to:

    `https://msdn.microsoft.com/en-us/library/ms244709.aspx`

Summary

In this chapter, we learned to create basic SQL reports using Report Builder and Report Designer. In the next chapter, we will learn about Team Web Access reports.

Team Web Access Reporting

Team Web Access reporting in TFS is basically constructed to manage and view reports and track status and information regarding project activities. Team Web Access, which is associated with the team project portal, is defined for the team project collection in TFS or Visual Studio Online. Team Web Access provides the easiest way to plan and track the progress of the project by managing source code, work items, and test efforts.

This chapter covers the following topics:

- Team web access levels
- Team web access charts
- Team web access standard reports

Team web access levels on TFS hosted as on-premise deployments require providing access levels to a group of users to features and reports in team web access as per the license level. Some of the features such as team rooms, authoring charts, and test case management require an advanced access level. There are three access levels, basic, advanced, and stakeholders, that can be assigned to users or a group of users using the TFS Administrator role.

For more information about the Visual Studio Online license and access level, have a look at following links:

- http://www.visualstudio.com/get-started/ assign-licenses-to-users-vsd
- http://www.microsoft.com/en-us/download/ details.aspx?id=13350
- http://www.visualstudio.com/products/compare- visual-studio-products-vs

Granting an access level to a user or a group of users

In order to have information and feature access based on access level, team members must have permission to the team project portal.

> For more information about permissions on the team project, have a look at following links:
>
> - `http://msdn.microsoft.com/en-us/library/bb558971.aspx`
>
> - `http://msdn.microsoft.com/en-us/library/dn249791.aspx`
>
> - `http://msdn.microsoft.com/en-us/library/hh562968.aspx`

The following steps are used to grant the access level to users or a group of users:

1. Open the TFS home page using TFS Administrator credentials. For example, go to `http://dipstfs:8080/tfs` and click on the Administrator Server setting button.

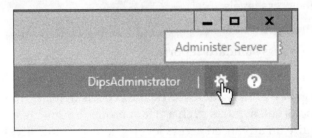

2. Go to the **Access levels** tab and choose a level:

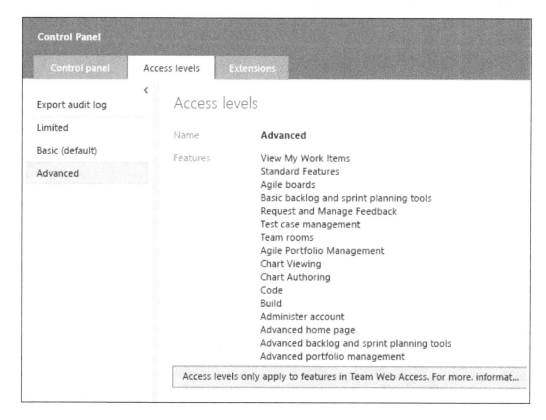

3. Click on **Add...** to assign users to the selected access level.

The basic access level

The basic access level requires the TFS client-access license. The basic access level has the following features:

- Managing work items in the product backlog:

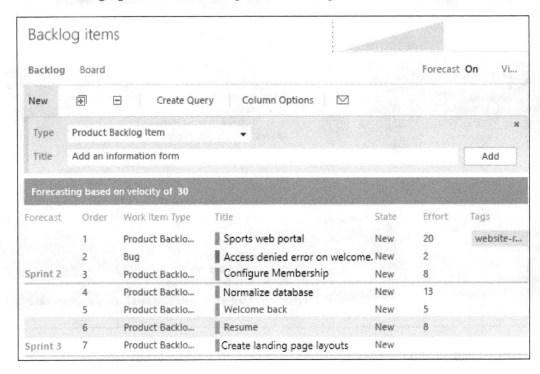

- Configuring sprints with product backlogs and task boards:

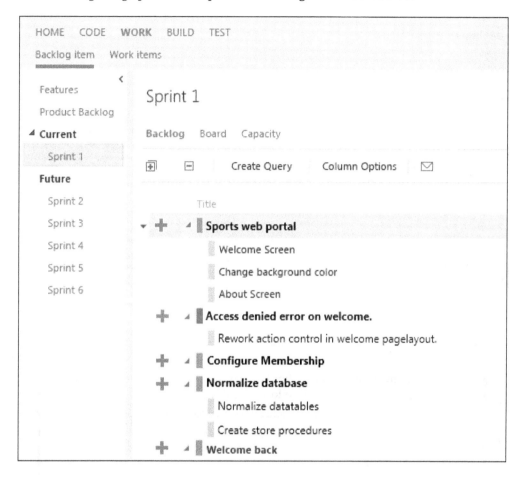

- Viewing work progress on the Kanban board:

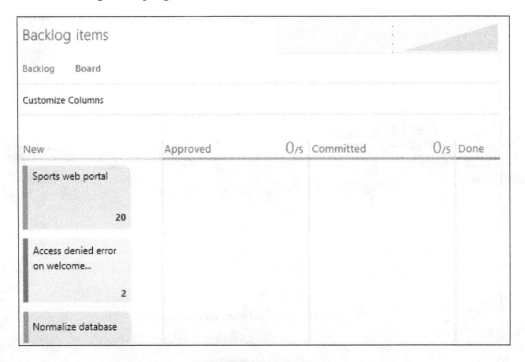

For more information about configuring the product backlog and sprints, have a look at following links:

- http://msdn.microsoft.com/en-us/library/ee518933.aspx

- http://msdn.microsoft.com/en-us/library/ee191595.aspx

- http://msdn.microsoft.com/en-us/library/jj838789.aspx

The advanced access level

The advanced access level requires MSDN subscription such as Visual Studio Ultimate with MSDN, Visual Studio Premium with MSDN/MSDN platforms, or Visual Studio Test Professional with MSDN. This access level includes the basic access level's features plus some additional features, which are as follows:

- Working with portfolio backlogs:

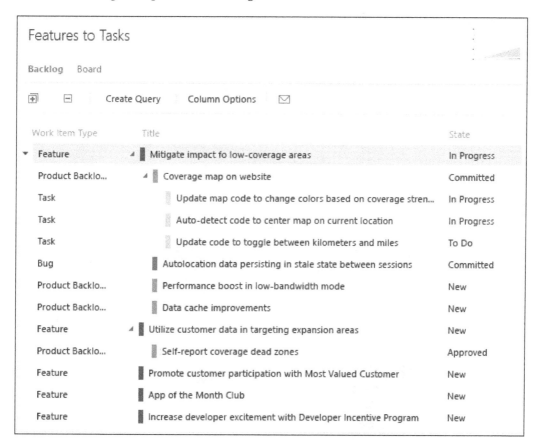

- Team room access

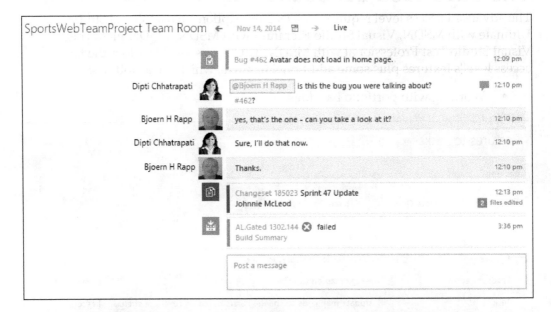

- Allowing the use of web-based test case management tools:

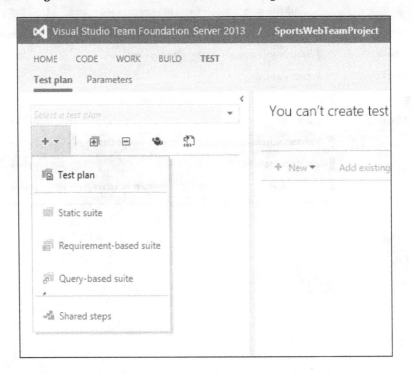

- Charting features to visualize the team progress:

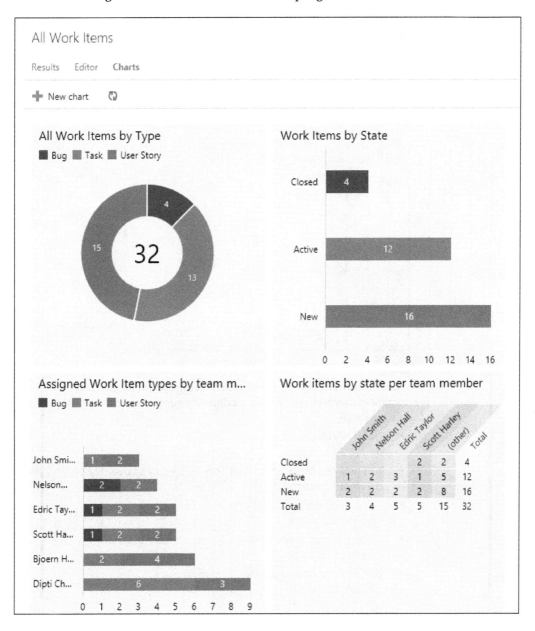

- Requesting and managing feedback from the customer:

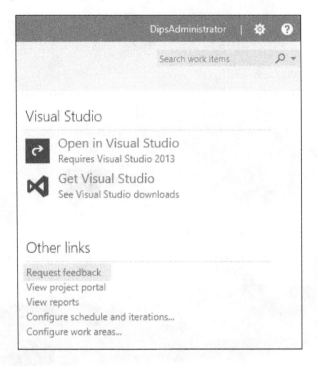

For more information about portfolio backlogs, team rooms, test case management, charting, and feedback requests, have a look at following links:

- `http://msdn.microsoft.com/en-us/library/dn237341.aspx`

- `http://msdn.microsoft.com/en-us/library/dn169471.aspx`

- `http://msdn.microsoft.com/en-us/library/dd380763.aspx`

- `http://msdn.microsoft.com/en-us/library/dn407521.aspx`

- `http://msdn.microsoft.com/en-us/library/hh301769.aspx`

The stakeholder access level

The stakeholder access level does not require any license. With this access level, users can access team project home pages, portfolio backlogs, and other backlogs. They can view, create, and customize work items such as user stories, bugs, features, alerts, and feedback responses, as shown in the following screenshot:

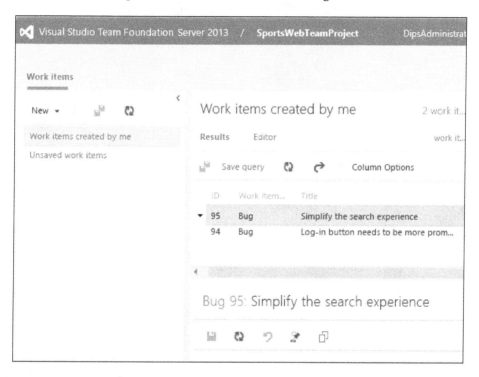

Team web access charts

TFS 2013 has introduced a new lightweight reporting feature called **Work Item Charting** that enables team members to create charts from the results generated by a work item in a flat query list. Work item charting allows visualizing work progress via various charts such as pie charts, column charts, or trend charts.

This feature is available in on-premise TFS as well as Visual Studio Online. The following section illustrates how to create and customize the chart on the team project's web access portal.

The following steps will walk through how to add and customize the chart:

1. Open the team project portal site and select a relevant query, for example, a query that fetches all work items. Click on the **Queries** tab and go to **New | New query**, as indicated in the following screenshot:

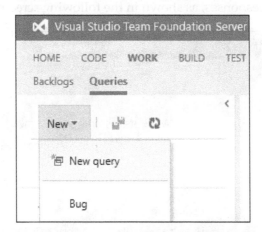

2. Save the default query as **All Work Items**.

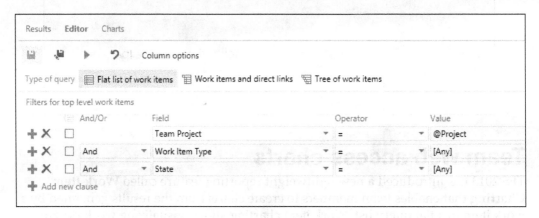

3. Click on **Charts**:

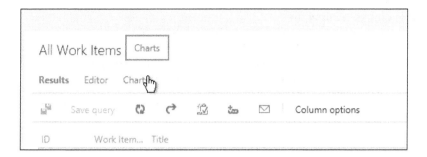

4. Click on **New chart**:

5. Group by **Work Item Type**:

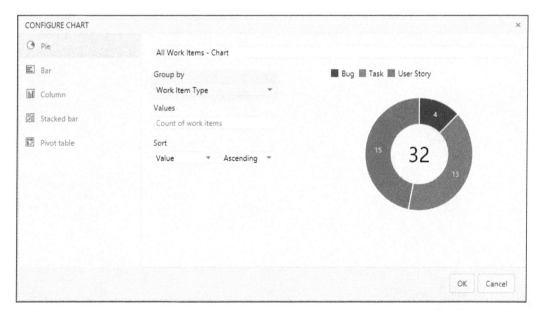

As indicated in the preceding screenshot, there are many types of charts available: pie charts, bar charts, column charts, stacked bar charts, and pivot table charts, as specified on the left pane.

6. To view a **Bar** chart and **Column** chart, you have to select the type accordingly from the left panel and specify the **Group by** field. The following bar chart illustrates all work items assigned by states:

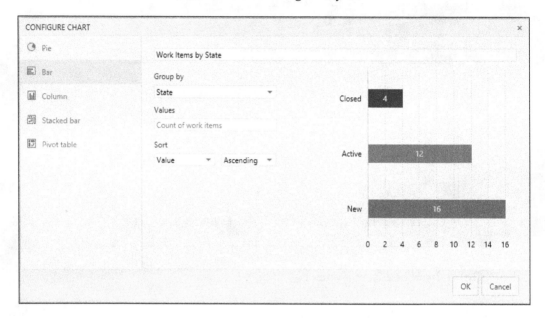

The column chart will look like this:

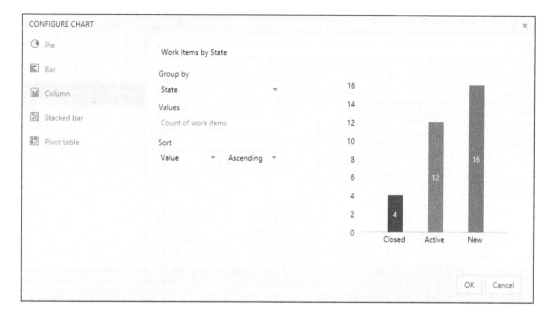

7. To view a **Stacked bar** chart and **Pivot table** chart, select the type accordingly from the left panel and specify values for **Rows** and **Columns**. The following stacked chart illustrates assigned work item types per team member:

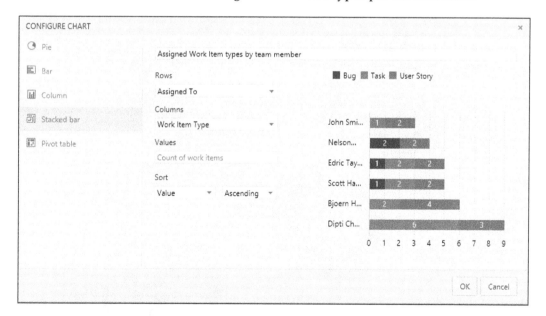

The following pivot table chart illustrates work items by state per team member:

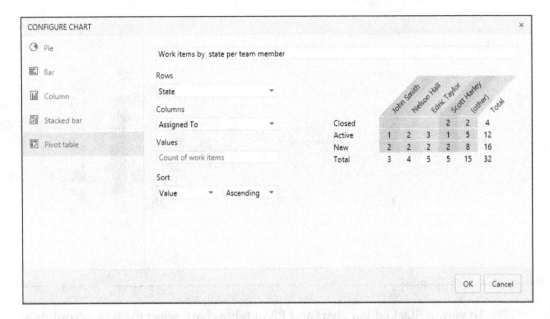

8. After choosing the desired chart and options, click on **OK** and the chart will appear in the **Charts** section; it can be edited later if neccesary:

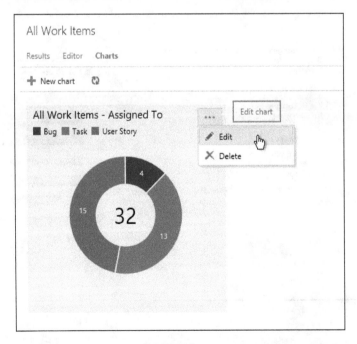

9. Add further charts using the **New chart** button that allows various charts on the same page to provide a clear view of the team's work. The following chart section represents various chart types for different views:

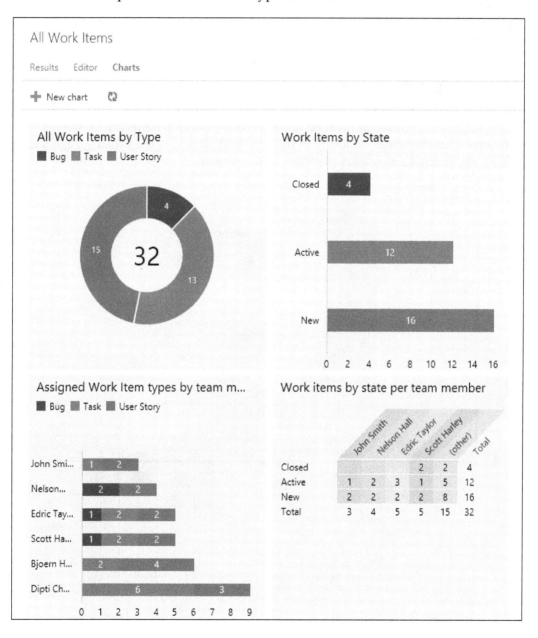

Team web access standard reports

Team web access has some useful built-in reports that can't be customized. However, these reports do not depend on the SQL Reporting service, and reports are available on Visual Studio Online too. The next section explains available standard reports in team web access.

The velocity report

The velocity report is used to forecast backlog accomplishment per sprint. This report shows the number of finished and scheduled backlog items across sprints/iterations. This report can be found in the top-right section of the backlog page and helps with forecast and release planning of the project.

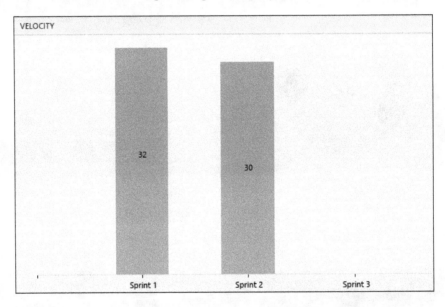

The cumulative flow report

The cumulative flow diagram shows up to 30 weeks of data, displaying the number of work items and their states according to the date range, as indicated in the following screenshot:

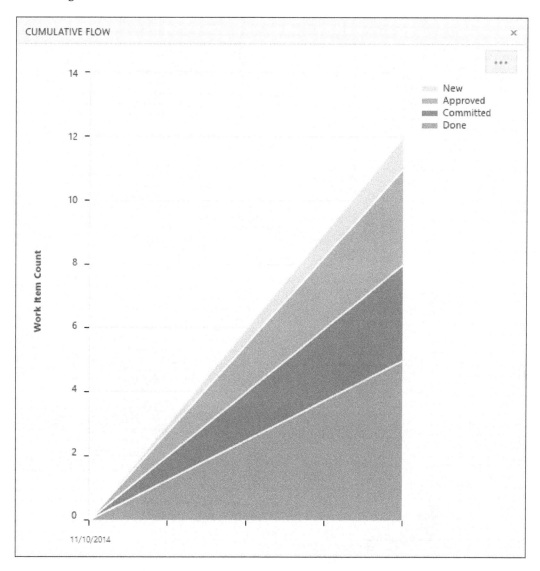

The sprint burndown report

Finally, the Sprint Burndown report shows the total number of hours that the team planned for the sprint. As the team's work gets completed, the value for the remaining work on the *y* axis will change and the trend line will forecast work completion based on the current work rate.

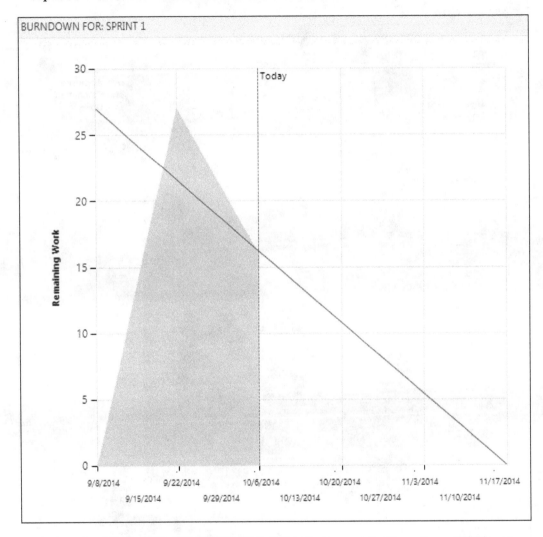

For more information about team web access standard reports, have a look at following links:

- `http://msdn.microsoft.com/en-us/library/dn283465.aspx`
- `http://msdn.microsoft.com/en-us/library/jj838789.aspx`
- `http://msdn.microsoft.com/en-us/library/ee191595.aspx`

Summary

In this chapter, we reviewed team web access levels and their various features based on need and walked through a very light feature called work item charting. Also, we discussed inbuilt standard reports.

At the end of this chapter, we saw different types of TFS reports and their features; however, TFS also has its own **TFS API** in order to create more customized reports. For example, you can create a TFS work item with about three lines of C# code. You can also use the TFS API to create reports in a supported way. There is also the **REST API** released for TFS to allow clients to be created for tablets, on Microsoft Windows operating systems, and smartphones insofar as they support HTTP requests.

However, at present, this API is only available for Visual Studio Online; it is expected to be available for on-premise deployments in a later version of TFS.

Index

A

access level
  advanced access level 119-122
  basic access level 116-118
  granting 114, 115
  stakeholder access level 123
  team project, URL 114
advanced access level
  about 119
  features 119-122
  team project, URL 122
agile process planning
  reference link 4
ALM
  about 1
  and TFS 2013 6
  core practices 6, 7
  references 9
  with business trends 8, 9
analysis service cube 16
Azure 2

B

basic access level
  about 116
  features 116-118
  team project, URL 118
Bug Backlog Management Excel reports
  about 49, 50
  Bug Progress report 50, 51
  Bug Reactivations report 56, 57
  Bugs by Assignment report 54-56
  Bugs by Priority report 53, 54
  Bug Trends report 52, 53

Bug Progress report
  about 50
  characteristics 50, 51
Bug Reactivations report
  about 56
  characteristics 56, 57
Bugs by Assignment report
  about 54
  characteristics 54-56
Bugs by Priority report
  about 53
  characteristics 53, 54
Bugs Dashboard
  reference link 50
Bug Trends report
  about 52
  characteristics 52, 53
Build Management Excel reports
  about 58, 59
  Build Status report 62, 63
  Code Churn report 60, 61
  Code Coverage report 59, 60
BUILD-MEASURE-LEARN cycle 8
Build Reports 78
Build Status report
  about 62
  characteristics 62
Build Summary report
  reference link 59
Build Verification Tests (BVT) 58
Burndown report
  about 44
  characteristics 44

C

CMMI 7
Code Churn report
  about 60
  characteristics 60, 61
Code Coverage report
  about 59
  characteristics 59, 60
core practices, ALM 6, 7
cumulative flow report 131
custom reports
  creating, Report Builder used 81-95
  creating, Report Designer used 97-111
Custom SQL Reports
  creating 80

D

dashboards
  about 35
  Bugs Dashboard 37
  Build Dashboard 37
  Burndown Dashboard 37
  My Dashboard 37
  Project Dashboard 37
  Quality Dashboard 37
  Test Dashboard 37
Default SQL Reports
  about 76-80
  Build Reports 78
  Project Management Reports 78
  reference link 79
  Test and Bug Reports 78
Direct Link Queries
  about 29-31
  URL 31

E

Excel reports
  about 16, 17
  creating 39
  creating, flat query list used 39-41
  prerequisites 36
  query-based reports, creating 41-43

F

Flat queries
  about 22-28
  URL 29

H

hybrid deployment 14

I

installation, SharePoint Server Enterprise Edition 36, 37
Issue Trends report
  about 48
  characteristics 48, 49

L

light weight reports 17

N

NT LAN Manager (NTLM) 39

O

operational stores 15

P

permissions, SharePoint 2013
  contribute permission 38
  read permission 38
PivotChart 35
PivotTable 35
prerequisites, Excel reports
  SharePoint 2013, integrating with TFS 2013 38
  SharePoint Server Enterprise Edition, installing 36, 37
  team project, provisioning with project portal 37
Project Management Dashboard
  reference link 49

Project Management, Excel reports
about 43
Burndown report 44
Issue Trends report 48, 49
Task Progress report 45, 46
User Story Progress report 46, 47
Project Management Reports 78
project portal
team project, provisioning 37

Q

Quality dashboard
reference link 59
query-based reports
creating, Excel used 41-43

R

relational databases 15
Report Builder
URL 76, 96
used, for creating custom reports 81-95
Report Builder 3.0
reference link, for setup 81
Report Definition Language (RDL) 73
Report Designer
about 16, 73, 76
URL 97
used, for creating custom reports 97-111
reporting tools
reference link 76
Report Server 75
report, types
about 17
Excel reports 17
light weight reports 17
REST API 18
SQL queries 18
SSRS reports 17
Team Web Access reports 17
TFS API 18
work item queries 17
work item reporting 17
REST API 18

S

Scrum 7
search box filtering
URL 22
Search Box Queries 21, 22
security 16
Shared Queries 23
SharePoint 2013
integrating, with TFS 2013 38
mandatory permissions, for integrating
with TFS 2013 38
SharePoint Server Enterprise Edition
installing 36, 37
Sprint Burndown report
about 132, 133
reference link 133
SQL Reporting Service Reports 74
SQL Server Report Builder 73
SQL Server Reporting Services 73, 74
SQL Server Reporting Tools
about 74, 75
Report Builder 75
Report Designer 76
SSRS reports 17
stakeholder access level
about 123
features 123
System Integration Testing (SIT) 12

T

Task Progress report
characteristics 45, 46
Team Foundation Server. *See* **TFS**
team project
provisioning, with project portal 37
URL, for provisioning 38
team web access 113
team web access charts
about 123
adding 124-129
customizing 124-129
Team Web Access reports 17

team web access standard reports
  about 130
  cumulative flow report 131
  Sprint Burndown report 132, 133
  velocity report 130
Test Activity report
  about 69
  characteristics 69, 70
Test and Bug Reports 78
test case management
  reference link 5
Test Case Readiness report
  about 66
  characteristics 66, 67
  reference link 67
Test dashboard
  reference link 64
Test Failure Analysis report
  about 70
  characteristics 70-72
Test Management Excel reports
  about 63, 64
  Test Activity report 69, 70
  Test Case Readiness report 66, 67
  Test Failure Analysis report 70-72
  Test Plan Progress report 64-66
  User Story Test Status report 68
Test Plan Progress report
  about 64
  characteristics 64-66
  reference link 66
TFS
  about 1
  deploying, ways 10
  reference link, for reporting service 17
  URL 20
  URL, for configuration 38
  URL, for permissions 39
TFS 2013
  and ALM 6
  reporting service 15
  SharePoint 2013, integrating 38

TFS 2013 architecture
  about 10
  application tier 11
  build machine 11
  client side 10
  data tier 11
  hybrid deployment 14
  references 15
  TFS on-premises 10
  Visual Studio Online (VSO) 13
TFS API 18
TFS, basics
  about 2
  agile process, planning 3
  builds, processing 4
  reporting status 5
  team empowerment 2
  test cases, maintaining 5
  version control 3
TFS configuration settings,
    for Team Project 20
TFS Online 2
TFS reporting architecture
  about 15
  analysis service cube 16
TFS reporting architecture, components
  Excel reports 16
  operational stores 15
  relational databases 15
  Report Designer 16
  security 16
  warehouse adapters 15
Tree queries
  about 32, 33
  URL 33

U

User Acceptance Test (UAT) 12
User Story Progress report
  characteristics 46, 47
User Story Test Status report
  about 68
  characteristics 68

V

velocity report 130
version control
 reference link 3
Visual Studio 1
Visual Studio Online (VSO)
 about 2, 7, 13
 URL, for access level 113
 URL, for license 113

W

warehouse adapters 15
Work Item Queries
 about 20
 URL 21
work item reporting 17

Thank you for buying

Reporting in TFS

About Packt Publishing

Packt, pronounced 'packed', published its first book, *Mastering phpMyAdmin for Effective MySQL Management*, in April 2004, and subsequently continued to specialize in publishing highly focused books on specific technologies and solutions.

Our books and publications share the experiences of your fellow IT professionals in adapting and customizing today's systems, applications, and frameworks. Our solution-based books give you the knowledge and power to customize the software and technologies you're using to get the job done. Packt books are more specific and less general than the IT books you have seen in the past. Our unique business model allows us to bring you more focused information, giving you more of what you need to know, and less of what you don't.

Packt is a modern yet unique publishing company that focuses on producing quality, cutting-edge books for communities of developers, administrators, and newbies alike. For more information, please visit our website at www.packtpub.com.

About Packt Enterprise

In 2010, Packt launched two new brands, Packt Enterprise and Packt Open Source, in order to continue its focus on specialization. This book is part of the Packt Enterprise brand, home to books published on enterprise software – software created by major vendors, including (but not limited to) IBM, Microsoft, and Oracle, often for use in other corporations. Its titles will offer information relevant to a range of users of this software, including administrators, developers, architects, and end users.

Writing for Packt

We welcome all inquiries from people who are interested in authoring. Book proposals should be sent to author@packtpub.com. If your book idea is still at an early stage and you would like to discuss it first before writing a formal book proposal, then please contact us; one of our commissioning editors will get in touch with you.

We're not just looking for published authors; if you have strong technical skills but no writing experience, our experienced editors can help you develop a writing career, or simply get some additional reward for your expertise.

Team Foundation Server 2013 Customization

ISBN: 978-1-78217-714-2   Paperback: 102 pages

Learn how to customize TFS and create useful plugins for your organization

1. This book accelerates the understanding of TFS extension points.

2. Learn how to create a JavaScript web access plugin.

3. Discover the tips and tricks of customizing TFS.

Team Foundation Server 2012 Starter

ISBN: 978-1-84968-838-3   Paperback: 72 pages

Your quick start guide to TFS 2012, top features, and best practices with hands on examples

1. Learn something new in an Instant! A short, fast, focused guide delivering immediate results.

2. Install TFS 2012 from scratch.

3. Get up and running with your first project.

4. Streamline release cycles for maximum productivity.

Please check **www.PacktPub.com** for information on our titles

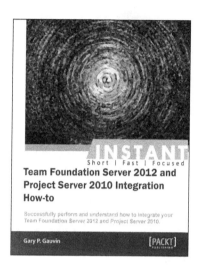

Instant Team Foundation Server 2012 and Project Server 2010 Integration How-to

ISBN: 978-1-84968-854-3   Paperback: 54 pages

Successfully perform and understand how to integrate your Team Foundation Server 2012 and Project Server 2010

1. Learn something new in an Instant! A short, fast, focused guide delivering immediate results.

2. Learn to plan and successfully implement your Team Foundation Server and Project Server integration.

3. Easily install or upgrade your Team Foundation Server extensions for Project Server.

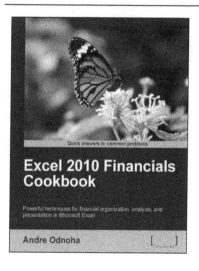

Excel 2010 Financials Cookbook

ISBN: 978-1-84969-118-5   Paperback: 260 pages

Powerful techniques for financial organization, analysis, and presentation in Microsoft Excel

1. Harness the power of Excel to help manage your business finances.

2. Build useful financial analysis systems on top of Excel.

3. Covers normalizing, analysing, and presenting financial data.

4. Clear and practical with straight forward, step-by-step instructions.

Please check **www.PacktPub.com** for information on our titles